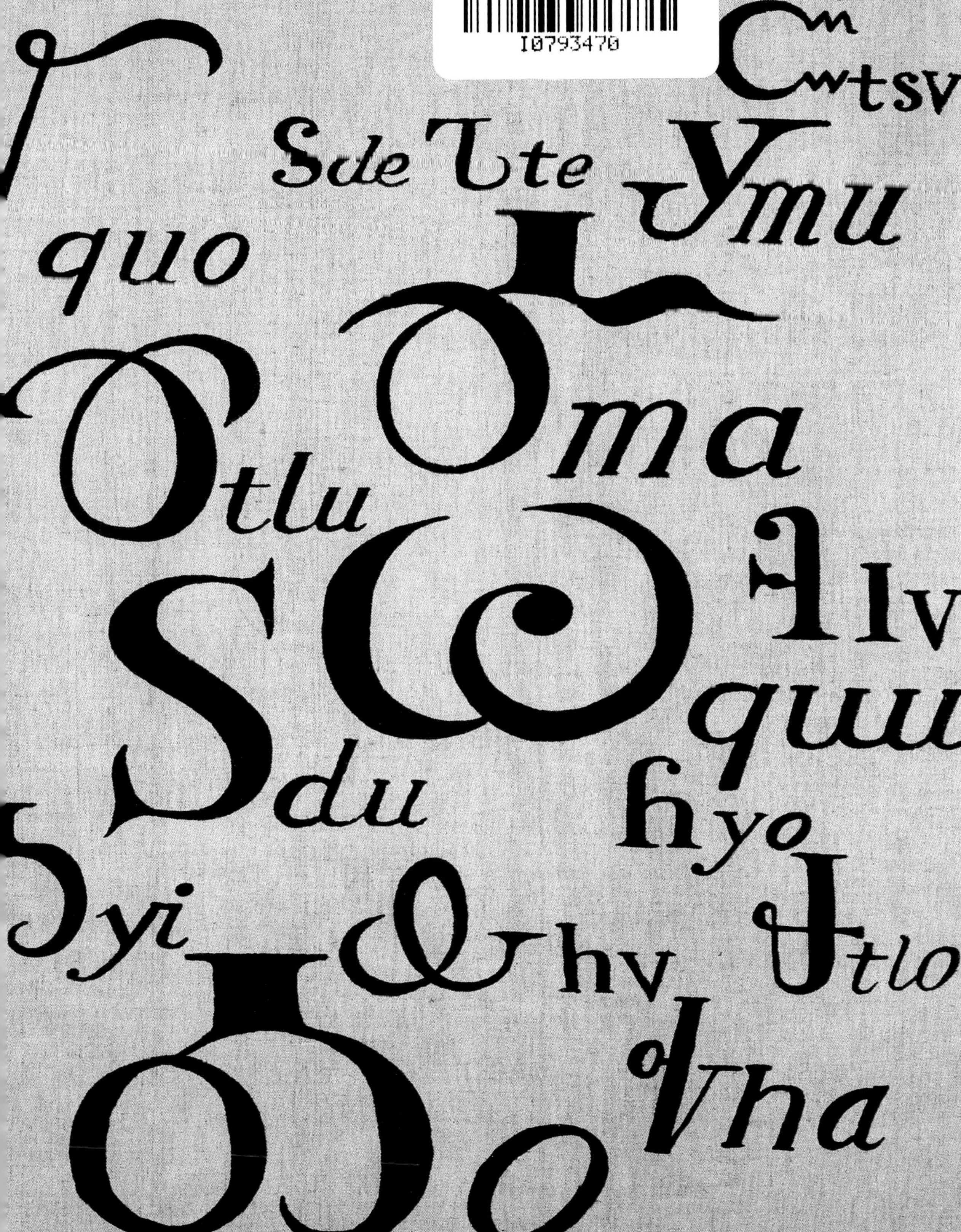

Lloyd Kiva New

Lloyd Kiva New

A New Century

The Life and Legacy of Cherokee Artist and Educator Lloyd Kiva New

Lloyd Henri New and a New Century
By Tony R. Chavarria, Curator of Ethnology
Museum of Indian Arts and Culture/Laboratory of Anthropology

Lloyd Kiva New: Art, Design, and Influence
By Ryan S. Flahive, IAIA Archivist; Rose Marie Cutropia, Independent Curator, and Tatiana Lomahaftewa-Singer, Curator of Collections, IAIA Museum of Contemporary Native Arts.

Finding a Contemporary Voice: The Legacy of Lloyd Kiva New and IAIA
By Carmen Vendelin, Curator of Art
New Mexico Museum of Art

Jhane Myers, Project Director
Museum of Indian Arts and Culture/Laboratory of Anthropology

Art Guild Press

Art Guild Press
PO Box 22651
Santa Fe, NM 87502
www.artguildpress.com

Printed in the United States of America

ISBN 978-0-9887791-5-0

Library of Congress Control Number: 2016954772

First Edition

Printed on 100# McCoy matte text. McCoy is made by Sappi in Cloquet, MN and boasts 10% post-consumer waste, FSC and SFI© chain of custody and SFI© fiber sourcing certifications. 100% of the electricity used to manufacture McCoy was generated with green-e© certified renewable energy.

On the cover: Lloyd Kiva New, *Indian Beadwork*. Photo by Jason S. Ordaz.

Inside: Lloyd Kiva New, fabric printed with Cherokee syllabary. Coutesy of Aysen New Collection. Photo by Walter Bigbee.

Contents

Dragonfly to the Sun

by N. Scott Momaday (Kiowa)

Great one,
Great giver of life and well being.
I lift my old arms in bold entreaty.
Rise and flood the land with light,
Rise and touch the faces of your people.
I entreat you, give us one more day,
And one more. And at last, one more.
I lift my old arms in bold entreaty.

Great one,
With respect I have breathed a smoke.
I have wreathed my words in wisps of smoke.
So it is they are made clean and strong.
With respect I have painted my face.
From my face come words of sacred color.
So it is they are made strong and beautiful.
I lift my old arms in bold entreaty.

Great one,
On the mountain you dance in whispering waters.
In the bear's tracks you pierce the darkness,
And you splinter among the limbs of pines.
The deer and the badger trace the arc of your path.
The prairie grasses tremble in your presence,
And now in the dawn appearing I summon you.
I lift my old arms in bold entreaty.

Preface

By David Warren, Ph.D. (Santa Clara Pueblo)

For nearly thirty years, David Warren, Ph.D. (Santa Clara Pueblo) held positions at the Institute of American Indian Arts as the Director of Curriculum and Instruction, Acting President and, later, the Director of the Cultural Research and Resource Development Center. In 1994, an award by the New Mexico Commission on Indian Affairs acknowledged his lifetime commitment to the preservation and perpetuation of American Indian languages and cultures.

> *The life story that follows is simply an account of one young person's struggle to find his way through the swirling entanglements of Indian/white identity problems, the strands of which at times seemed to form a kind of restrictive cocoon requiring a lifetime of struggling behavior to get the butterfly within to emerge. He was to learn, as innocence gave way to the realities of life, that the world operated very differently from the halcyon realm of Timber Hill secured by the heroic tales by his Cherokee mother and that there was a different life out there to be experienced before metamorphosed into the new form which would enable him to spread his wings and soar into the sunshine and fresh air of self-knowledge and happiness.*[1]
>
> *– Lloyd Kiva New*

The Institute of American Indian Arts (IAIA) is synonymous with revolutionizing Native American art, the formation of new genre. While Lloyd New is inextricably associated with that legacy, his place in its history should be more closely examined. Something else

1 Lloyd Kiva New, *The Sound of Drums: A Memoir of Lloyd Kiva New*. Ed. Ryan S. Flahive. (Santa Fe: Sunstone Press, 2016), 7.

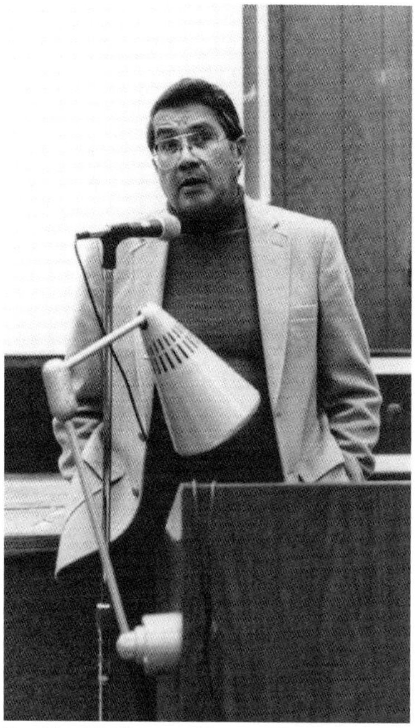

Dr. David Warren (Santa Clara Pueblo), c. 1975. Courtesy of IAIA Archives.

happened vast in its implications as an unprecedented, indeed historic, achievement in the history of Native American education.

For the first time, culture had been recognized as the core of an educational philosophy, pedagogy, and institution. It reversed centuries-long efforts to assimilate Indians into American society by any means possible. While more blatant, the now infamous comments of the Superintendent of Carlisle Indian School, Captain Richard Pratt, "kill the Indian and save the man," had continued unabated as a principle in Native educational philosophy and programs for over a century. Eradicate all that constituted the vital identity of a person and place in its stead another self that was not him nor could it ever be so.

IAIA was criticized in its early days by collectors and galleries as a betrayer of valid, legitimate Indian art. For those who defined valid Indian art as ethnographic, the Institute was producing works so avant-garde as to be unrecognizable. Ironically, what they wanted was a Native person who was the perpetuation of something that Pratt had wanted to destroy.

While others viewed the new art as inauthentic, Lloyd saw the work as an evolution of Indian art originating from the flow of Indian life itself. It simply represented a phase in the continuum of Native culture, or "Indianness," as he called it.

It was apparent that old paradigms of education for this generation were unacceptable and obsolete. And it was the arts as manifestations, expressions, and demonstrations of culture that Lloyd recognized as the foundation of a new philosophy and innovative educational institution.

The challenge was daunting; but the conditions were not unfamiliar to Lloyd. The opening passage of this preface from his memoirs, *The Sound of Drums*, recollects events that transcended his life, remembering and recasting his ideal of Cherokee being and spirit. No matter that the culture was severely shattered over years of programmed detribalization and deculturation. What came of the experience are principles that guided the rest of his life.

Around 1982 Lloyd wrote,

> *...the Indian must live in two worlds. Our students, especially those of the 1960s, were acutely aware of life in this interim status and in that time of social protest ambience created even greater stress as many sought some classic moment in their own tribal memory as a stabilizing point. Indianism was the center point of the Institute curriculum. It was carefully structured and nurtured...it was essential that the sense of cultural identity be protected as its natural development be fostered in a total program of study and training... we held that Indian youth must be taught to respect and cherish the unique qualities of his own culture and how to build on them. He must be taught to view with understanding and regard the various values of diverse cultures...he must be trained to assess objectively all of this accumulated knowledge so that ultimately he would be prepared to select those values which, for him, would serve as the foundation for a constructive life.*[2]

When Lloyd wrote of "Indianism," I think he was recasting traditional Indian art not merely as a repository for past ideas and images, but rather as a foundation for creating new, ever-changing expressions of a vital culture. "Every student should know his own distinct cultural heritage...learning to link the best in Indian culture to contemporary life, [a student]...will be able to solve his own problems and enrich the world scene in the process."[3]

2 Lloyd Kiva New, "The Institute of American Indian Arts and Its Significance in the Development of Modern Indian Art," (Santa Fe, c. 1982), 12-13.

3 Lloyd H. New, report submitted to the Special Sub-Committee on Indian Education, U.S. Senate Committee on Labor and Public Welfare, "The Role of the Institute of American Indian Arts in the Development of Indian Education and Its Potential as a Major Cultural Institution," (Santa Fe, 1969), 3.

Lloyd's intuitive genius in cultural approaches to Native education take on even greater significance when one compares his ideas to the theories of Calvin Taylor, Howard Gardner, Rudolf Arnheim, and Edward T. Hall, all central figures in research on educational psychology, creativity, and the culture of education. What they postulated was actually taking place at IAIA in studios, classrooms, student living, and cultural events.

This was especially revealing with Harvard psychologist Jerome Bruner. In his *Culture of Education*, Bruner described culture as the essence of what constituted being human. For him, culture shaped the mind; it provided the way for us to conceive of who we are and what our potential for development may be. Moreover, it was essential that culture's integrity and stability be maintained in order to fully develop our potential as human beings. He suggested that differing Native talents existed, that it was important to respect the special nature of identities tied to our communities and experience. Individuals, therefore, construct knowledge on the basis of their culture and from their own experiences.[4]

Bruner's studies and Lloyd New's concepts were mirror images. It is not surprising, therefore, that the Institute's design was foremost a response to the individual student. There, students found an ambience of education and learning that fostered exploration and establishment of identity on one's own terms. It was a self-discovery process that manifests itself in new art.

IAIA responded to a calling at a critical time in Native American history. In a sense, the story represented the long-standing conflict found in all study and interpretation of Native people, one of a constant question of authority and authentication. But Lloyd articulated these issues so clearly, using art as a grand metaphor, in describing the change as inevitable, perhaps necessary for a new generation to find its way.

The Institute was at the nexus of a new history characterized by public awareness of culture. It is culture, the means by which we make meaning of the world, and the force that defines self and community—

4 Jerome Bruner, *The Culture of Education*, (Cambridge, MA: Harvard University Press, 1997).

and completes the total and essential function of life. Deeply innate values and beliefs have transcended countless efforts to alter, diminish, or destroy their essence.

Today, the social and cultural context of Indian education is once again changing. We stand at the threshold in American Indian development. A new process of identity-making is also shaping itself. Repatriation of cultural patrimony, tribal language, and the restoration of traditional homelands are shaping a process that can be called true community building in every aspect, especially culture.

Paradoxically, Lloyd was a man of his time, yet he anticipated a means to restore culture as part of a process in a setting that many may have thought was impossible. Many now remark of his place in their lives; helping to clear their own paths, create their own visions, and build a fulfilled life. He may indeed be a mentor to a generation. He found a way to demonstrate that we learn in a multiplicity of ways, but most of all, our capability and ability to learn must come from a deep and abiding pride, meaning self-respect, in who we are.

This was the life of Lloyd New, the legacy we now honor.

Introduction

By Della Warrior (Otoe-Missouria Tribe)
Director, Museum of Indian Arts and Culture / Laboratory of Anthropology

Too often an individual's creativeness and passion for pursuing that creativity is not acknowledged and overlooked. The contributions that individuals have made go unrecognized and undocumented. One such individual was Lloyd Kiva New, a humble Cherokee man, a great educator, an artist, fashion designer, leader, mentor and visionary. Lloyd set the pace for changing the landscape of Native American art. He threw down the gauntlet and challenged all to open their minds to their own creativity and to utilize their talents to the maximum extent. Lloyd Kiva New was an amazing man who paved the way for Native youth to become the very best contemporary artists and to be leaders in their field. He was a key advisor to numerous boards, museums, and individuals.

This catalog celebrates the life of Lloyd Kiva New on what would have been his 100th birth year. It is produced through a collaboration between the Museum of Indian Arts and Culture (MIAC), the IAIA Museum of Contemporary Native Art (MoCNA), and the New Mexico Museum of Art (NMMOA) in Santa Fe, New Mexico. Each museum installed a unique and distinct exhibition memorializing the life and work of Lloyd Kiva New. The MIAC exhibition is entitled: *A New Century: The Life and Legacy of Cherokee Artist and Educator Lloyd Kiva New*; the title of the IAIA MoCNA exhibition is: *Lloyd Kiva New: Art, Design, and Influence*; and the NMMOA exhibition is entitled *Finding a Contemporary Voice: The Legacy of Lloyd Kiva New and IAIA*. The curators of these three exhibitions highlight their respective exhibitions within the content of this book.

We wish to thank Mrs. Aysen New, Lloyd's widow, for her instrumental role in advancing the concept for an exhibition commemorating the life of Lloyd Kiva New. It has been a pleasure working with our colleague institutions as well as the Museum of New Mexico Foundation. The curators of the exhibitions, Tony Chavarria, Ryan Flahive, Tatiana Lomahaftewa, Rose Marie Cutropia, and Carmen Vendelin deserve the highest commendations for their outstanding work. We truly are grateful for the support of individual sponsors for the exhibitions and for the grant from the Santa Fe Arts Commission. Thanks to Shelley Thompson and Eric Davis for all of the great publicity the exhibitions received. Special thanks also to Dr. N. Scott Momaday, Dr. Nancy Mithlo, and Dr. Dave Warren for their contributions to this publication. Lastly, but critically important, we would like to acknowledge and thank Robert Erlichman, the publisher of this catalog.

Lloyd Kiva New was a wonderful person and a brilliant man. He was a mentor to thousands of students and an advisor to numerous Native cultural institutions. His influence and leadership are renowned and will resonate throughout Indian Country for generations. We are proud to honor him and his legacy through the exhibitions and this catalog on the centennial year of his birth. Lloyd was, without a doubt, a Grandfather to both Native fashion and contemporary Native art.

I would like to acknowledge and thank my partners in this unique collaboration for taking a leadership role in honoring Lloyd: Dr. Robert Martin, President of the Institute of American Indian Arts, Mary Kershaw, Director of the New Mexico Museum of Art, and Patsy Phillips, Director of the IAIA Museum of Contemporary Native Arts. With these three institutions collaborating we were able to celebrate the legacy of Lloyd Kiva New in an outstanding manner to which this book is a testament. We hope you enjoy this catalog.

A Brief Biography of Lloyd Kiva New

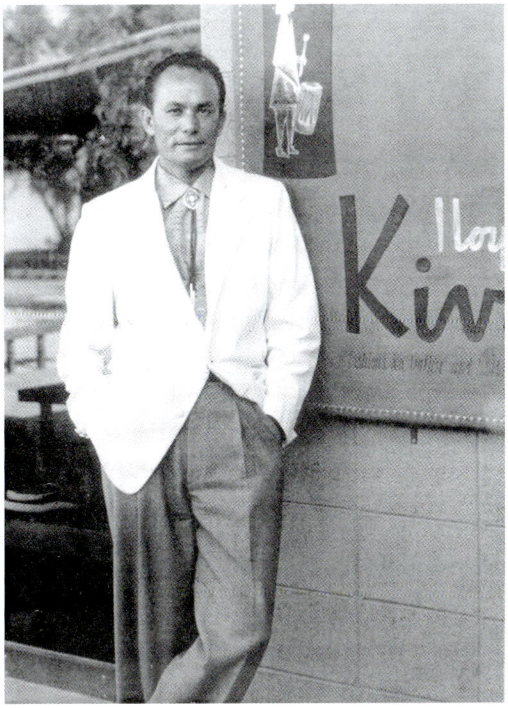

Lloyd Kiva outside of his shop in Scottsdale, Arizona. Courtesy of Lloyd H. New Papers, IAIA Archives.

Lloyd Henri New, known professionally as Lloyd Kiva New, was a man of many interests and talents. From his early years as a student at the Art Institute of Chicago, Lloyd New held a deep and abiding appreciation for both his Cherokee and his Scots-Irish cultural heritage. His personal history, along with a familiarity with modern educational philosophies, provided a foundation for his lifelong interest in Native American arts education.

Lloyd New began his academic career as a teacher at the Phoenix Indian Boarding School from 1939-1941 after which he served in the United States Navy during World War II. In 1946, New began a business and career as a fabric manufacturer, fashion designer, and property developer at the Kiva Crafts Center in Scottsdale, Arizona.

In 1958, Mr. New continued his academic career as a director of the Southwest Indian Arts and Crafts Workshop in conjunction with the University of Arizona. This was a ground-breaking program focused on contemporary Native American arts training sponsored by the Rockefeller Foundation.

In 1961, New was hired by the Bureau of Indian Affairs as the first Art Director for the newly established Institute of American Indian Arts (IAIA) in Santa Fe, New Mexico, where he helped develop an indigenous arts curriculum. In 1967, New became the Institute's President and remained in that position until his retirement in 1978.

Between 1978-1988, Lloyd Kiva New was a dynamic member of several arts and museum boards including the U.S. Department of Interior's Indian Arts and Crafts Board and the Native American Center for the Living Arts (The Turtle Museum) in Niagara Falls, New York. In 1988, New again influenced the focus and direction of IAIA, serving as Interim Director during a period of reorganization under a new Congressional non-profit charter of 1986.

From 1989-2002, Lloyd Kiva New was a world-renowned Native American arts consultant and conference speaker. His influence inspired and helped to shape such highly acclaimed organizations as the Smithsonian Institution's Gustav Heye Center in New York City and the National Museum of the American Indian in Washington, D.C., as well as the Plains Indian Museum at the Buffalo Bill Historical Center in Cody, Wyoming. A staunch advocate of IAIA throughout his lifetime, New was also a pivotal member of the IAIA Foundation Board of Directors from 1990-1999.

Some of Lloyd New's awards and honors are the American Craftsmen's Council Southwest Regional Merit Award in the Field of Printed Textiles; the American Institute of Decorators Certificate for Design Associate (1960); the University of Arizona's Medallion of Merit (1960); the American Institute of Interior Designer's Certificate for Fabric Manufacture (1962); New Mexico Arts Commission Board Member (1966-1971); American Council for the Arts in Education Award (1974); American Crafts Council Fellow (1976); American Indian National Achievement Award in Art Education (1976); Santa Fe "Living Treasure" (1989); Santa Fe Mayor's Recognition Award for Excellence in the Arts (1992); IAIA Museum Welcoming Circle Dedication (1992); U.S. Department of the Interior Recognition Certificate for New's work on the Indian Arts and Craft Board (1993); Red Earth magazine's "Honored One" (1994); IAIA Foundation Visionary Award (1996); Harold W. McGraw, Jr. Prize in Education (1997); Lovena Ohl Foundation Award (1998); 26th Annual Governor's Award for Excellence in the Arts Individual Support for the Arts through Education (1999); IAIA Honoring Ceremony (2000); Arizona American Indian Tourism Association's Red Tuxedo Honoree (2001); and the IAIA Lloyd Kiva New Endowed Chair in Design and Applied Arts (2004).

A biography of Lloyd Kiva New is not complete without noting his wide-ranging intellectual and academic interests and his work in Native American arts education framing the innovative program at IAIA. His perspective on the critical link between culture, self-identity, and self-determination produced philosophical writings on multicultural education and its importance to Indian art, education, and museum development. For more information about Lloyd Kiva New, visit his personal papers at the IAIA Archives in Santa Fe, New Mexico.

Lloyd Henri New and A New Century

By Tony R. Chavarria, (Santa Clara Pueblo) Curator of Ethnology
Museum of Indian Arts and Culture/Laboratory of Anthropology

Indian art of the future will be in new forms, produced in new media and new technological methods. The end result will be as Indian as is the Indian.

– Lloyd Kiva New

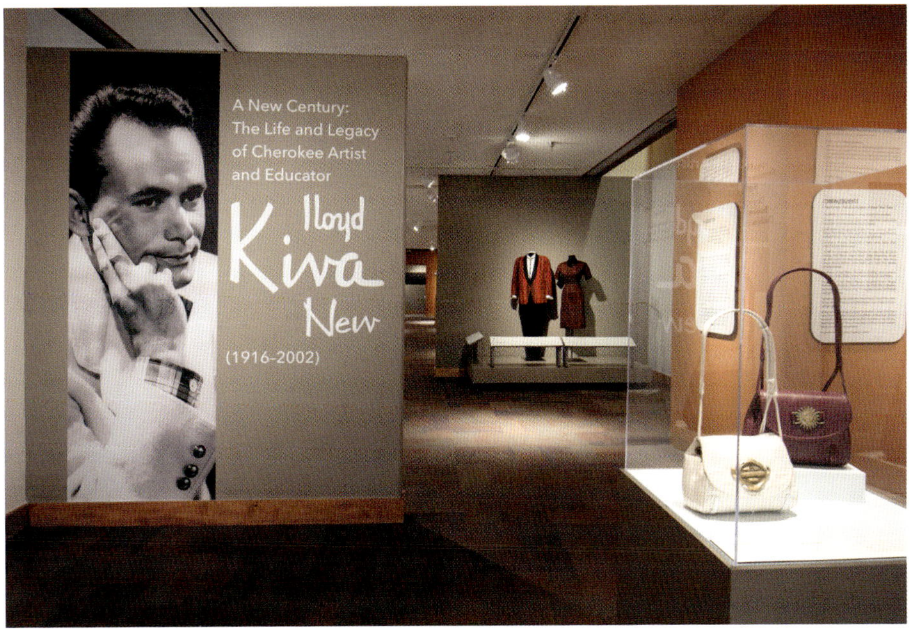

A New Century at the Museum of Indian Arts & Culture, Santa Fe, NM, 2016. Photo by Blair Clark.

A *New Century: The Life of Cherokee Artist and Educator Lloyd Kiva New*, at the Museum of Indian Arts and Culture, commemorates the 100th anniversary of the birth of a Native pioneer in fashion design, entrepreneurship, and cultural art education. He blazed a trail that many are just beginning to tread. Throughout his story we see correlations between his career and the history of the Cherokee people.

Thanks to Lloyd's widow, Aysen New, we have access to a treasure trove of writings, photographs, sketches, and artwork, much of which has never been seen publicly. Using this wealth of material, *A New Century* examines Lloyd Kiva New's life through photographs, fashions, documents, and art. Through multiple meetings with Mrs. New, we discussed and developed a story about Lloyd and his myriad contributions to Native art and culture. We encapsulated that story in four sections in the gallery.

"Oklahoma" traces New's roots on the hardscrabble family farm where he grew up and shows how his life of daily chores and listening to Cherokee stories from his mother set a foundation of artistic and intellectual pursuit. "Student, Teacher, and Sailor" looks at his time as a student at the Chicago Art Institute and as a young art teacher in the American Southwest until he served in the U.S. Navy during World War II. "A New Enterprise" tells of how handbags and clothes made the man known as Lloyd Kiva. And "New Horizons and the New Legacy" tells of how he left his successful entrepreneurial ventures and came to the Institute of American Indian Arts to pursue his vision of new methods in Native art education.

> *I always say that you can't teach innovation, but he (Lloyd New) knew how to identify talent, nourish it, and allow it to become.*
>
> *– Marcus Amerman (Choctaw)*

Due to the inherent limitations of space within an exhibition setting, many details are summarized or omitted. What is left is hopefully a still illuminating portrait of a man with a vision.

For me, it has been revealing to research the writings and documents and conjecture about what his priorities and dreams were at these different stations in life. In a sketchbook dating to his student years, New ruminated on sweethearts and art. Some of these are so privately expressive that I am only comfortable acknowledging their existence, but not their content. I came across a handwritten draft resume from later on in which he was already stressing his experience with American Indian art education; here he mentioned the Laboratory of Anthropology, although he didn't discuss it in detail. Luckily, these clues have allowed archivists Diane Bird of the Laboratory of Anthropology, Ryan Flahive of the Institute of American Indian Arts, and researcher Elizabeth Murphy to find more information about this early period, to the benefit of grateful curators and future researchers.

Unearthed documents now confirm Lloyd's presence at the Lab, the Santa Fe Indian School, and the University of New Mexico in the late 1930s. It was at this time that Lloyd Henri New (the "Kiva" would be added later) first met Dorothy Dunn. These two preeminent figures in American Indian art education had diametrically opposite teaching philosophies, yet both were committed to the sharing Native art and culture with the world.

> *And while everyone knows that the world of fashion is indeed strange and capricious, it nonetheless represents one of the most basic and compelling impulses, from the simplest to the most complex of cultural enclaves – each has engaged in one form or another in the art of personal adornment.*
>
> *– Lloyd Kiva New*

According to New's memoirs, his formative years in Oklahoma were at the forefront of his mind later in life. It is typical, when one has led a storied life, to look back more often than forward, but I believe that there was more to this than nostalgic recollection. New's childhood experiences led to a lifelong examination of what being Cherokee

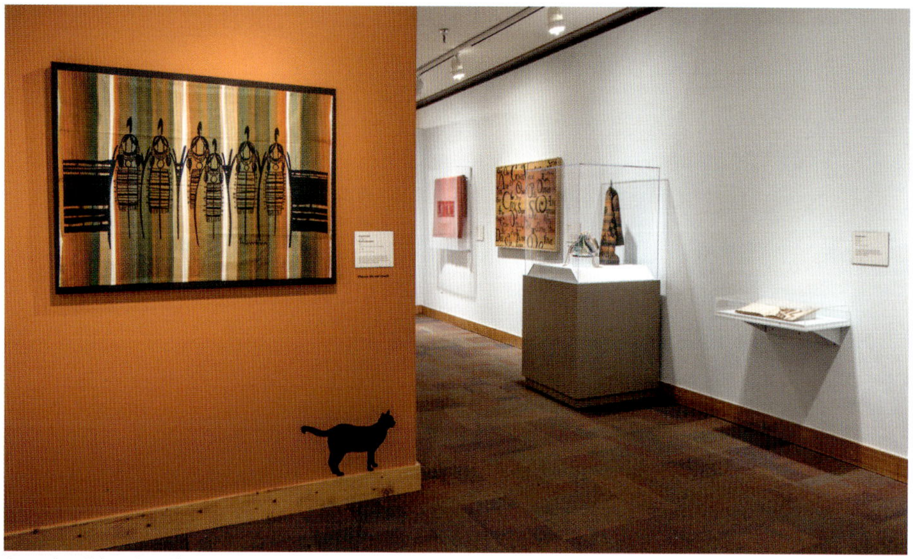

A nod to Lloyd and Aysen's cat, Lui, in *A New Century*. Photo by Blair Clark.

meant to him as a person and to his people. In so doing, he repeatedly drew correlations between his career and the cultural history of the Cherokee people.

New seems to have believed that much of the pre-European contact cultural practices of Oklahoma Cherokees were lost as a result of the forced relocations of the early 1800s. The uprooting of a people from their traditional homelands in the east to Indian Territory was devastating, since traditions and language are so strongly linked to place. As a result of this upheaval, new practices and traditions evolved, with echoes of the past, to reflect their new place of being. By adapting to new physical and ethereal environments, Cherokees were able to survive and, eventually, to thrive. This is reflected in New's story.

New's life was shaped by finding his way from the Oklahoma homeland to drastically dissimilar areas. In each of these areas, his ability to quickly adapt to previously unfamiliar lifeways and environments served him well. In each, his personal strength was abetted by a cultural practice; everywhere he went, he was able to find success. This is just one aspect of Lloyd Kiva New's life that has been illuminated in *A New Century*.

> *The creative genius behind what he (Lloyd New) did is not only in serving American Indian artists, but finding a way to look at the meaning of art and culture and put them into an institution and a philosophy.*
>
> *– Dave Warren, Ph.D. (Santa Clara Pueblo)*

In burgeoning post-World-War II Scottsdale, Arizona, Lloyd New established a boutique that focused on leatherwork and handbags. Finding quick success and a distinct branding sobriquet that referenced the region, "Kiva" bags became a sought after accessory for the well-heeled. Lloyd Kiva expanded his offerings to clothing and other accoutrements. The soon-to-be-renowned Hopi artist Charles Loloma designed many of the unique metal buttons, clasps, and medallions used on the Kiva brand clothing and handbags. In addition to Loloma, other native artists such as Manfred Susunkewa (Hopi), Larry Golsh (Pala Mission Band), and Andrew Van Tsinajinnie (Navajo) were hired to create designs for New's fabrics.

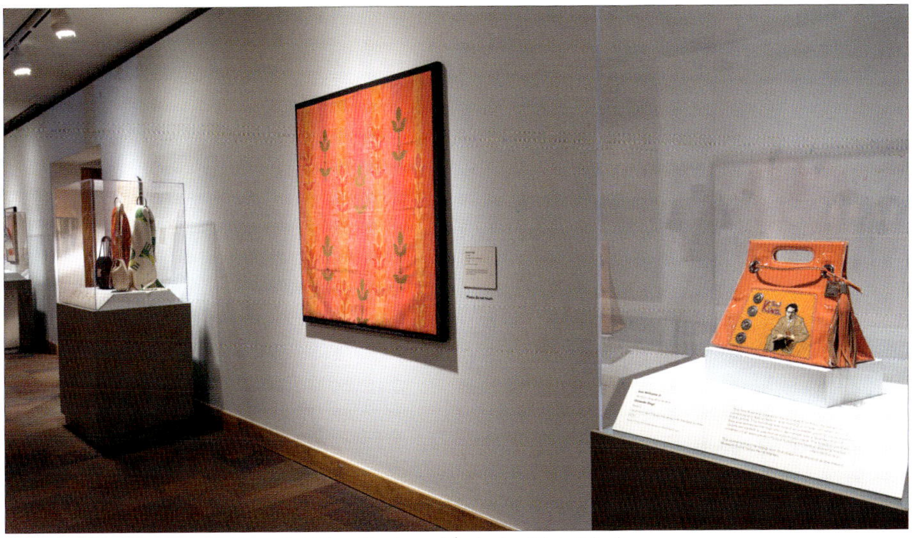

A view of the Legacy section of *A New Century*. Photo by Blair Clark.

During his days as a pioneering design entrepreneur, Lloyd New aspired to develop a center that would teach Indian students differently than government school settings. Other artists and educators were thinking along similar lines. This culminated in the establishment of the Institute of American Indian Arts (IAIA) in Santa Fe in 1962. Leaving the business of high fashion behind, Lloyd New would be IAIA's first art director and eventually president. Disillusioned by his experience with the Bureau of Indian Affairs (BIA), New wanted students to draw upon their cultural morés and aptitudes yet not be constrained by overly romantic or rigid teaching methods. He believed in creating and presenting art with integrity evolving from the students' growth.

Lloyd New's legacy as an educator lives on in the dynamic growth of IAIA and the decades of noted artists who studied there. His artistic and entrepreneurial visions endure in the ever expanding Native fashion movement. Contemporary artists such as Pilar Agoyo (Ohkay Owingeh / Santo Domingo / Cochiti) and America Meredith (Swedish / Cherokee) continue to cite New's significance. Today's Native art in its new forms and media, remains as Indian as the Indian. It is visible and relevant on a global scale in part due to the actions and innovations of Lloyd Henri Kiva New.

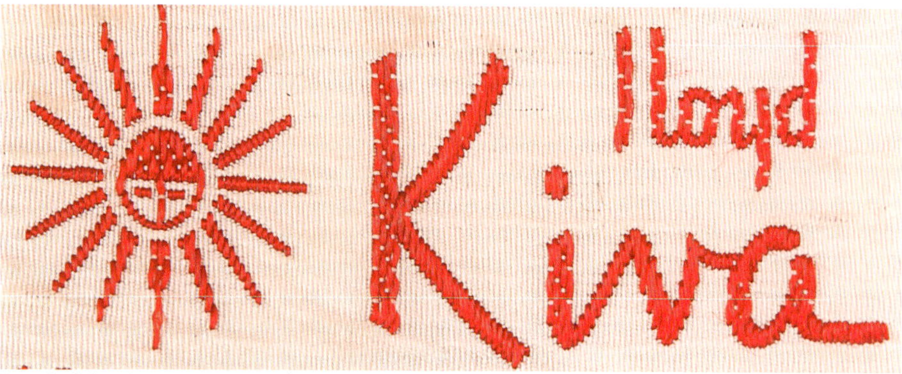

Detail of the Lloyd Kiva label. Photo by Blair Clark.

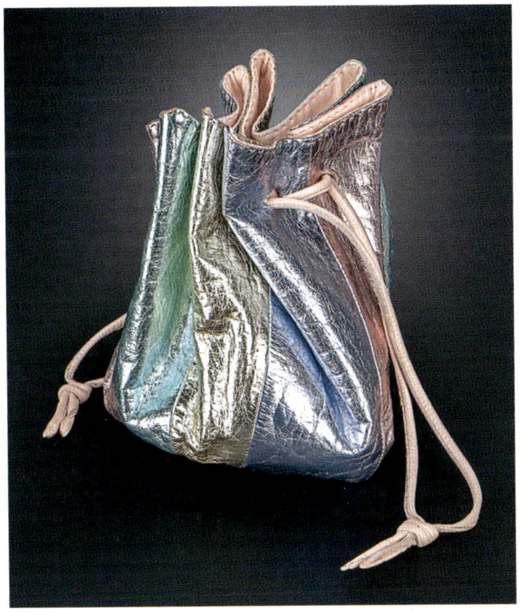

Kiva Lamé Handbag, c. 1956. Courtesy of Aysen New Collection. Photo by Blair Clark.

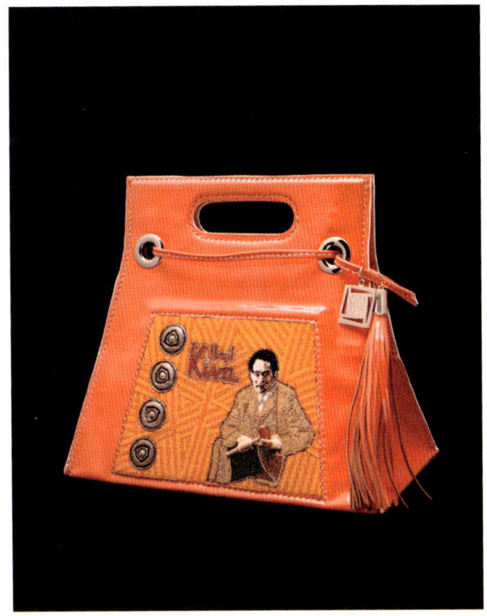

Lloyd Kiva New tribute handbag by Orlando Dugi (Navajo) and Ken Williams Jr. (Northern Arapaho/Seneca). Museum collection 59466/12. Photo by Kitty Leaken.

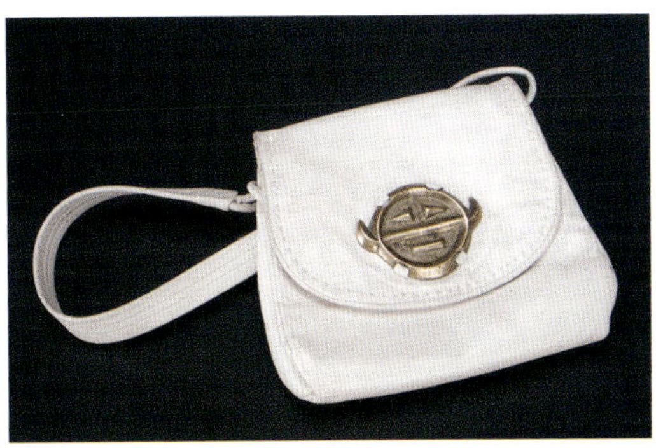

Kiva Handbag with Charles Loloma (Hopi) designed medallion, c. 1950. Courtesy of Aysen New Collection. Photo by Blair Clark.

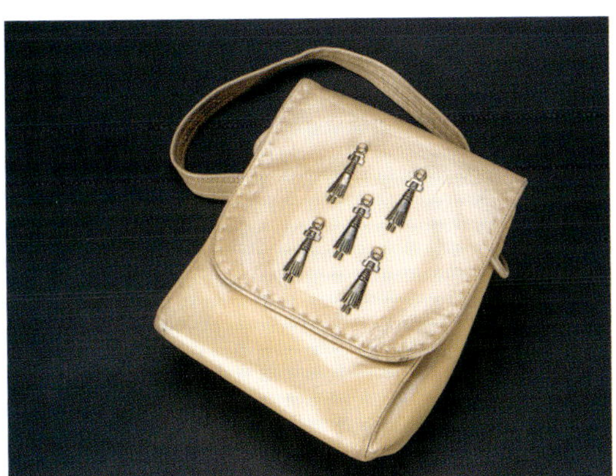

Kiva Handbag with Charles Loloma (Hopi) designed Shalako medallions, c. 1950. Courtesy of Aysen New Collection. Photo by Blair Clark.

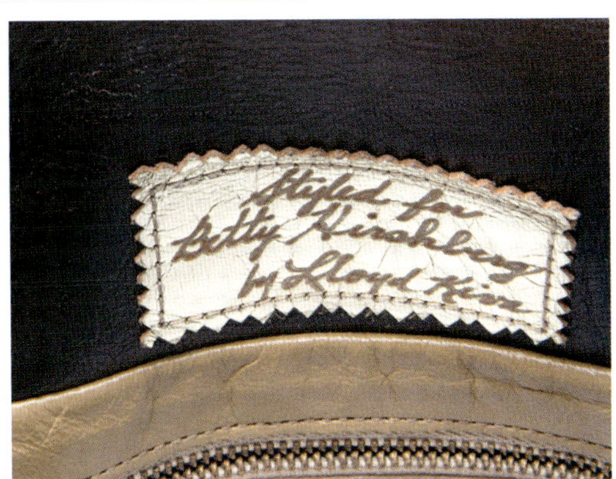

Detail of label found in Kiva bags to denote unique creations for each client. Photo by Blair Clark.

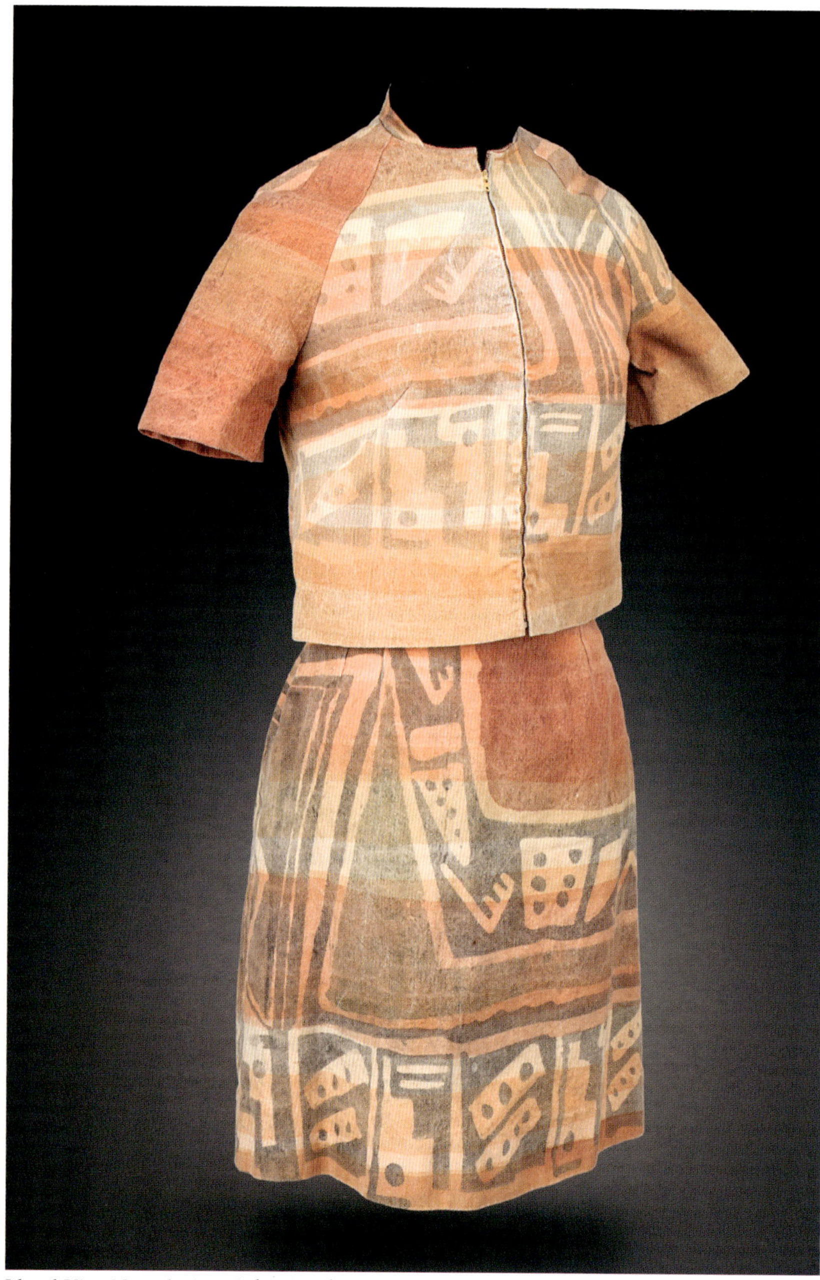

Lloyd Kiva New designed this Southwest-patterned ensemble; it dates to the early 1980s. Courtesy of Aysen New Collection. Photo by Blair Clark.

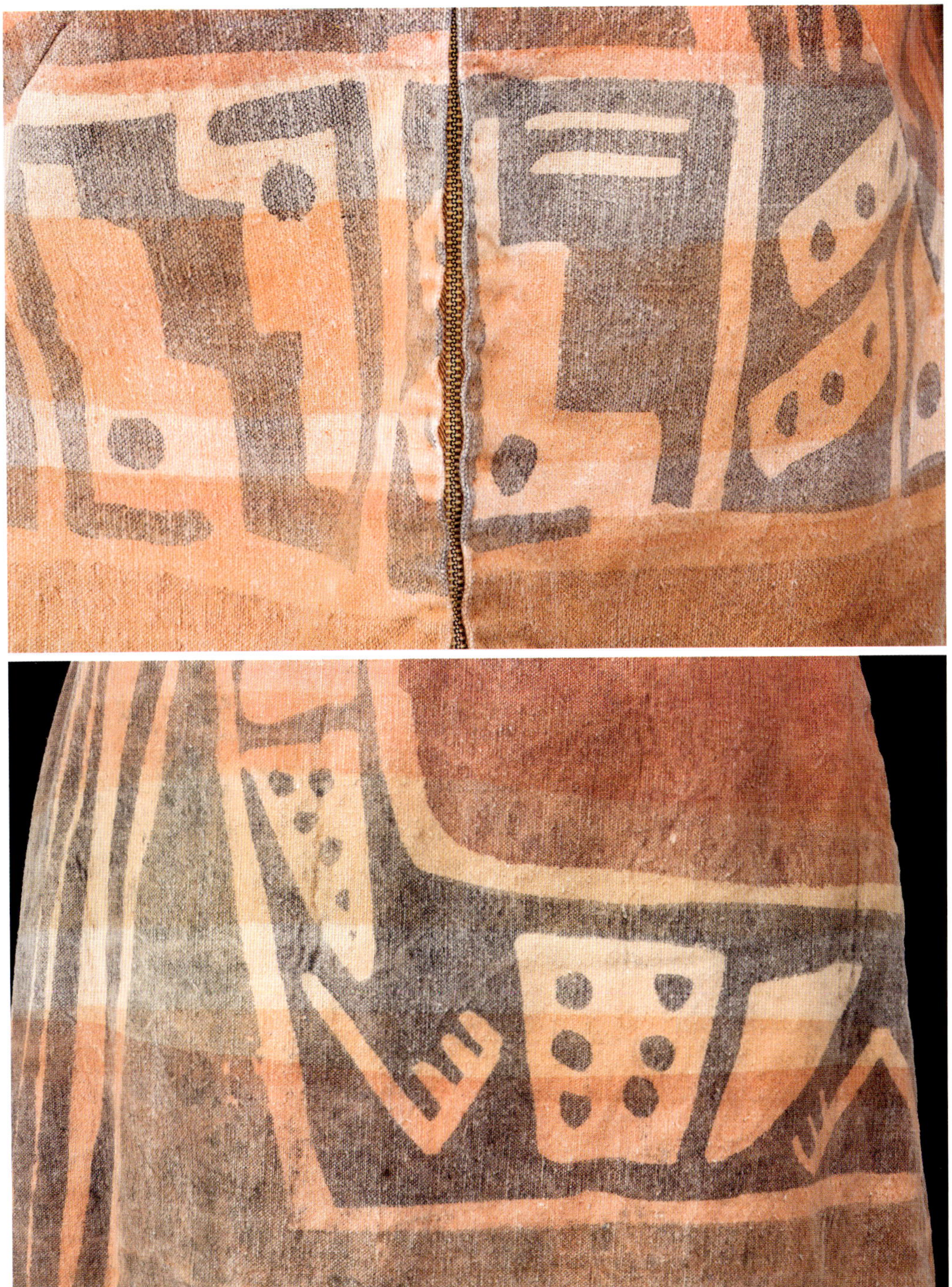

Details of dress on the facing page. Photos by Blair Clark.

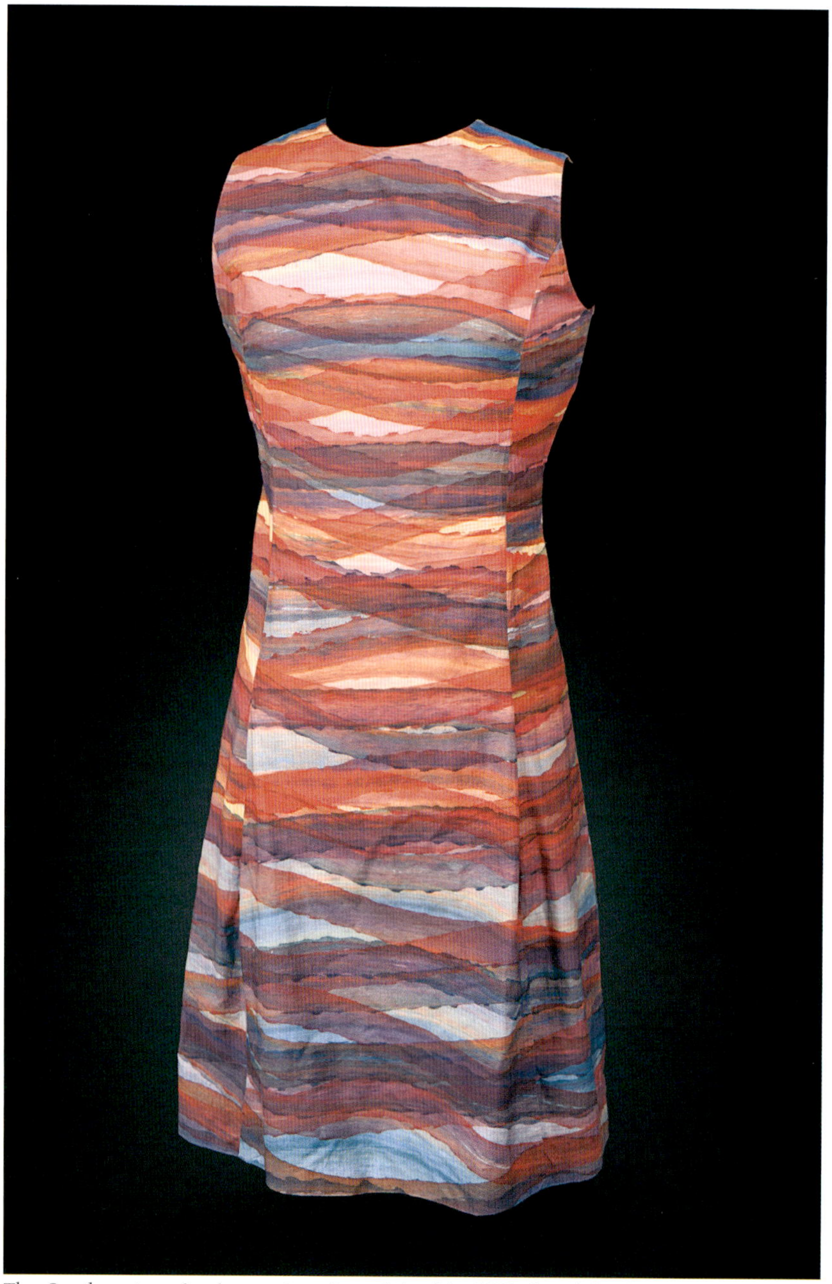

The Southwestern landscape is reflected in this 1950s hand-dyed, wool-jersey sheath. Courtesy of Aysen New Collection. Photo by Blair Clark.

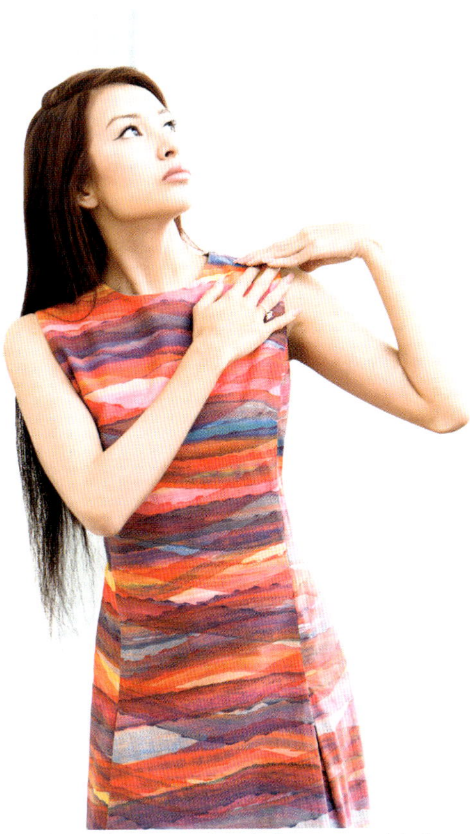

Lloyd Kiva landscape sheath dress as modeled by Wakeah, 2015. Photo by Kitty Leaken.

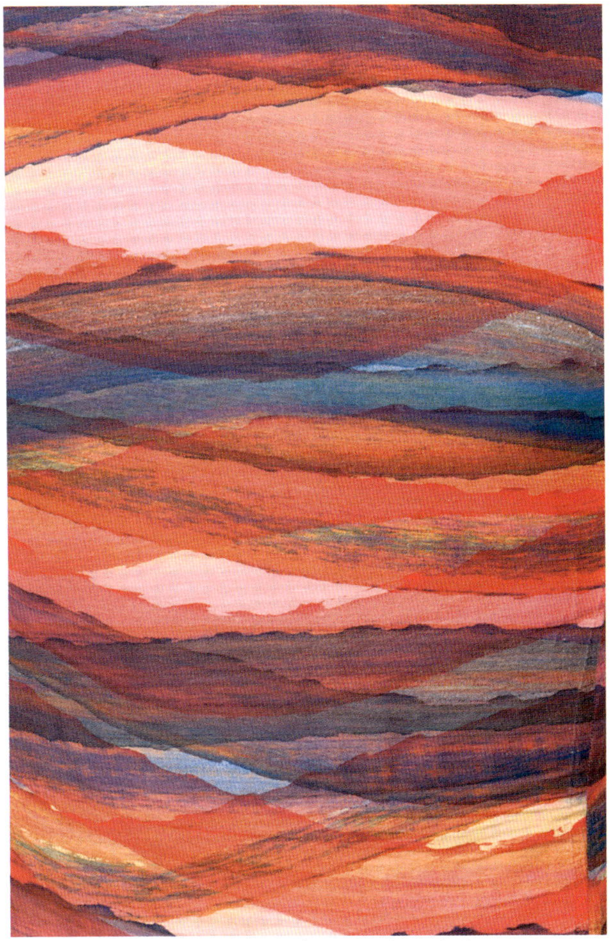

Detail of dress on facing page. Photo by Blair Clark.

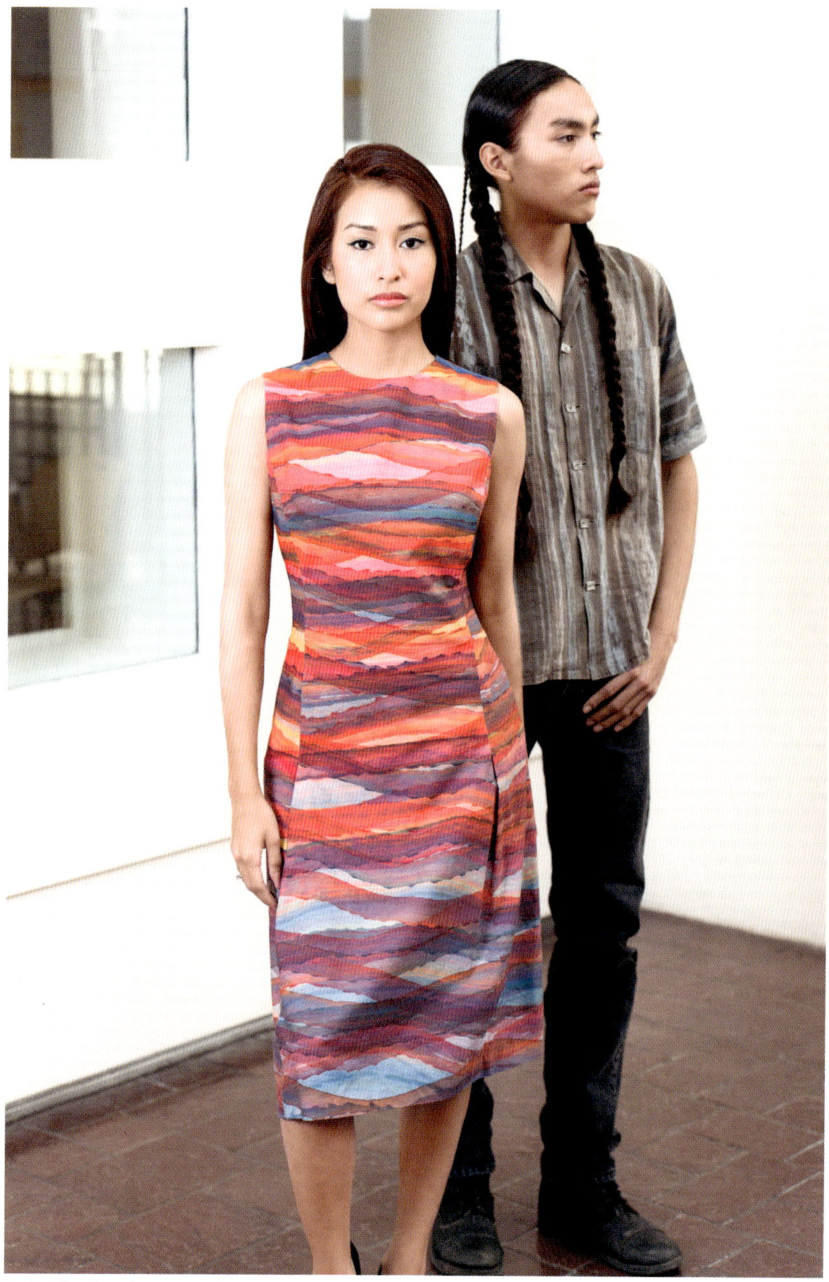

Left: The Southwestern landscape is reflected in this 1950s hand-dyed wool-jersey sheath. Right: This particular New-designed button-front shirt was worn by Lloyd Kiva New while he painted. Modeled by Wakeah and Phillip. Photo by Kitty Leaken.

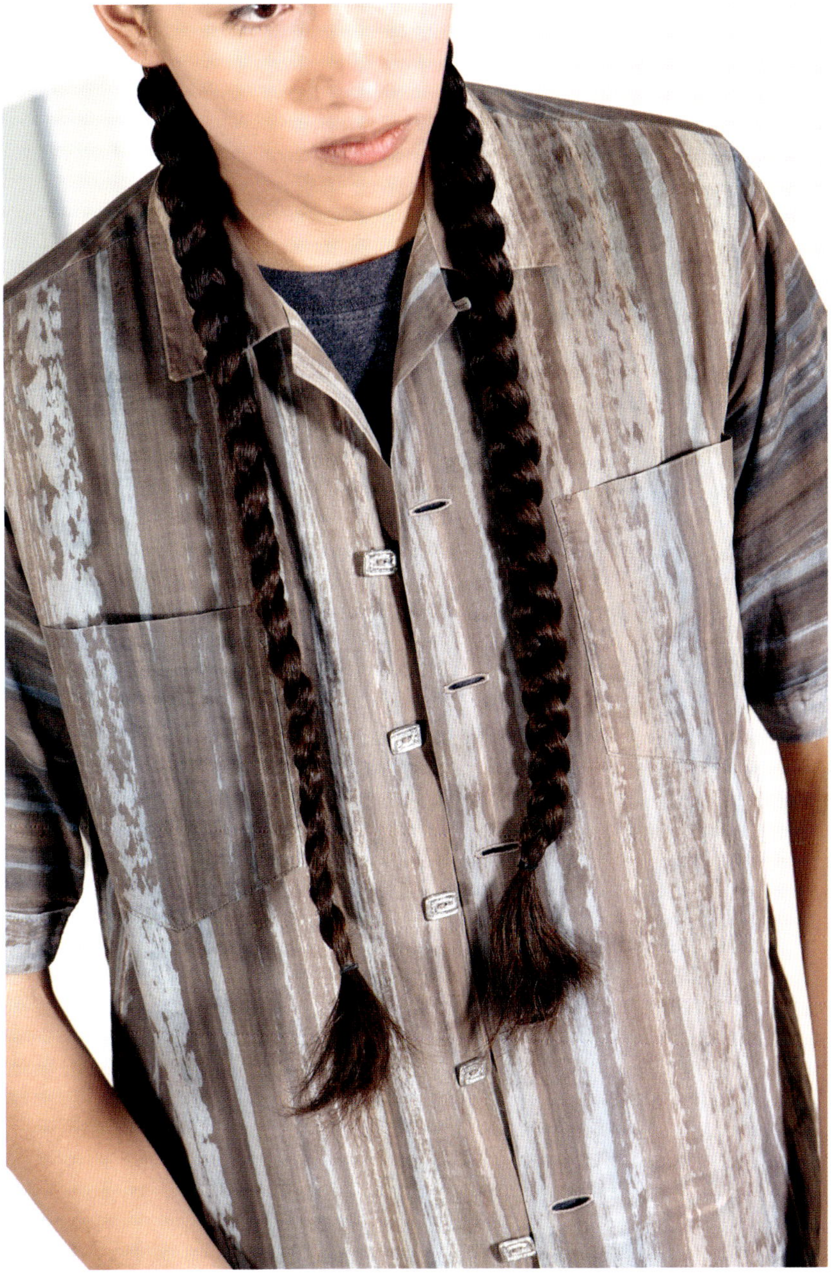

Phillip wearing a Lloyd Kiva New designed shirt with Charles Loloma (Hopi) designed buttons, c. 1960. Photo by Kitty Leaken.

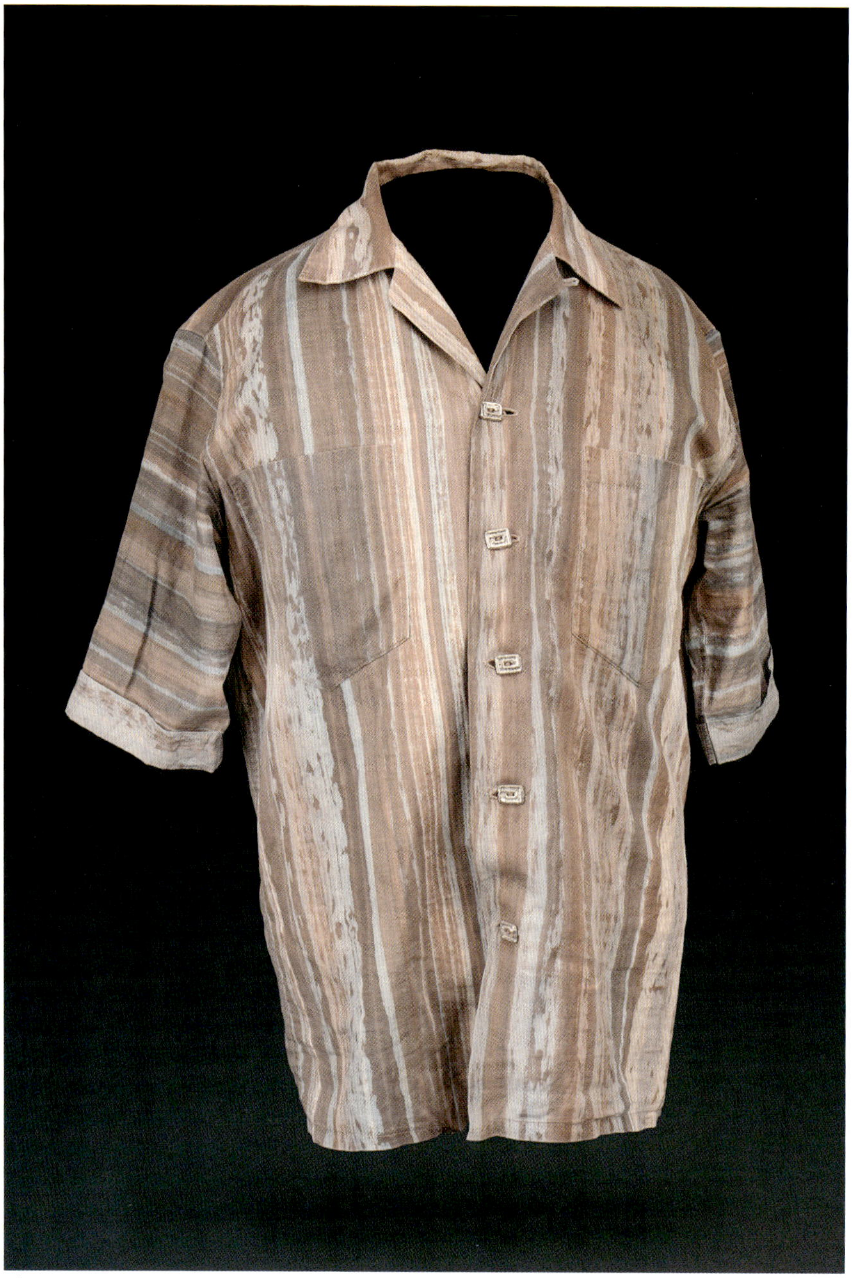

This particular New-designed button-front shirt was worn by Lloyd Kiva New while he painted. Courtesy of Aysen New Collection. Photo by Blair Clark.

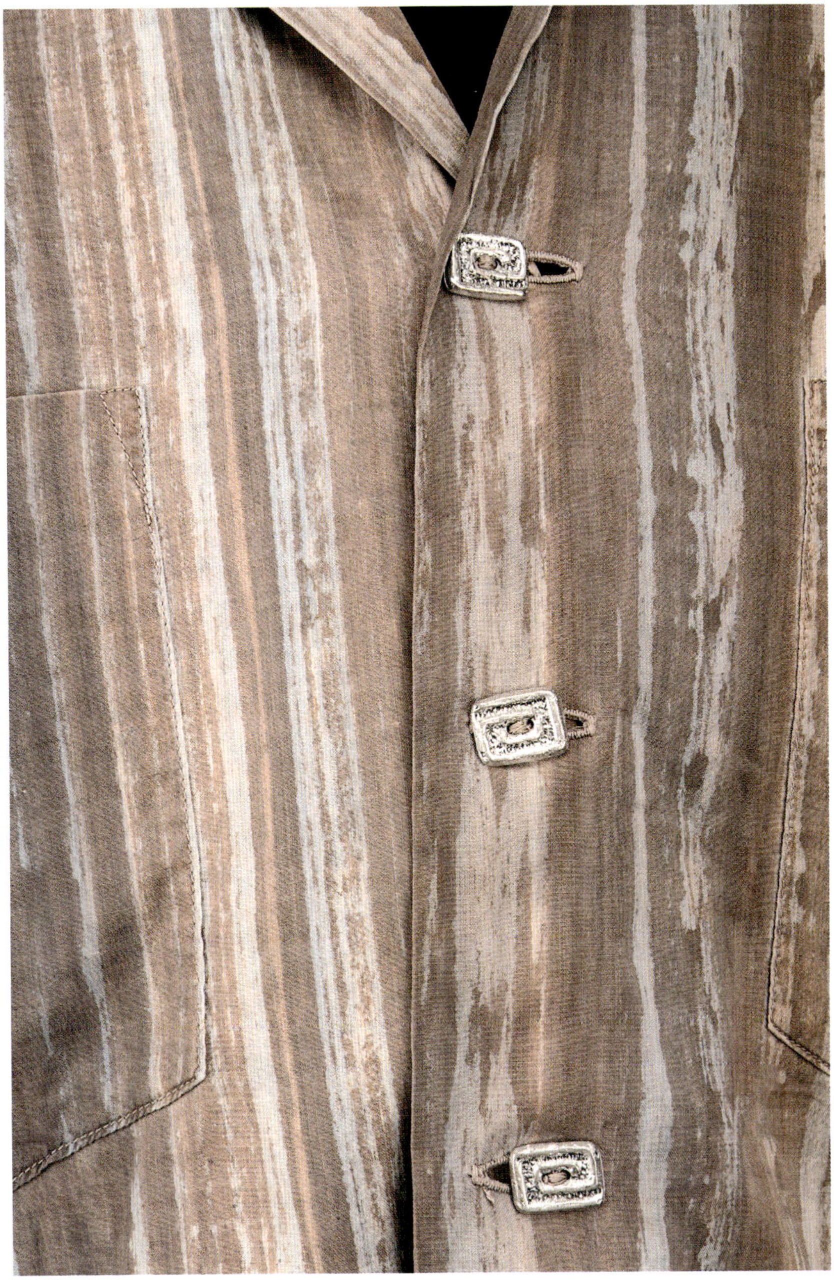

Detail of shirt on facing page showing the Charles Loloma (Hopi) designed buttons. Photo by Blair Clark.

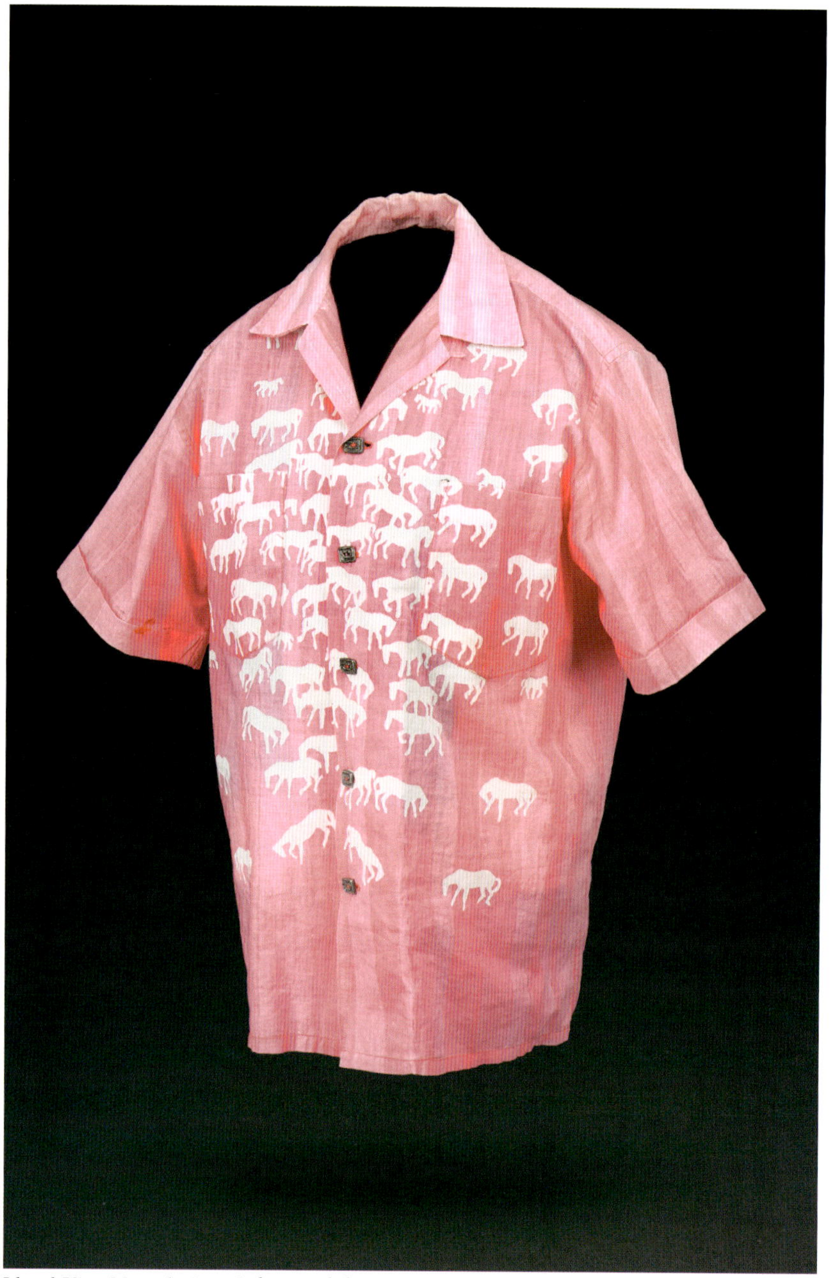

Lloyd Kiva New designed shirt with horse motif attributed to Andrew Van Tsinajinnie (Navajo), c. 1956. Courtesy of Aysen New Collection. Photo by Blair Clark.

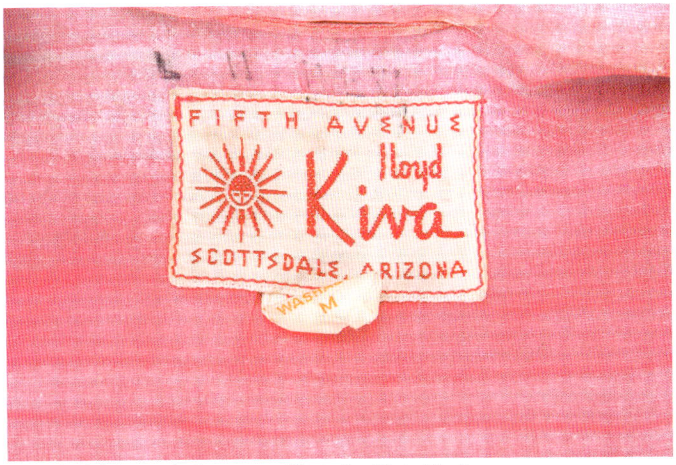

Detail of shirt on facing page. Photo by Blair Clark.

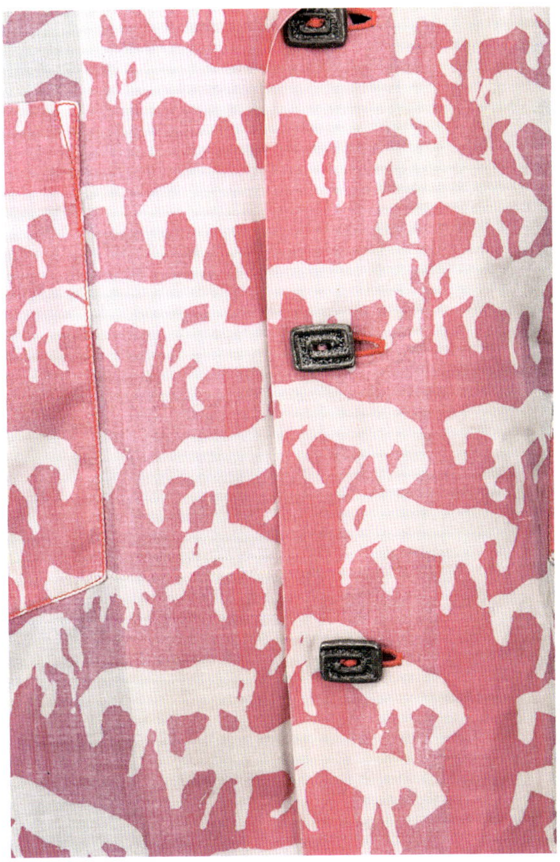

Detail of shirt on facing page. Photo by Blair Clark.

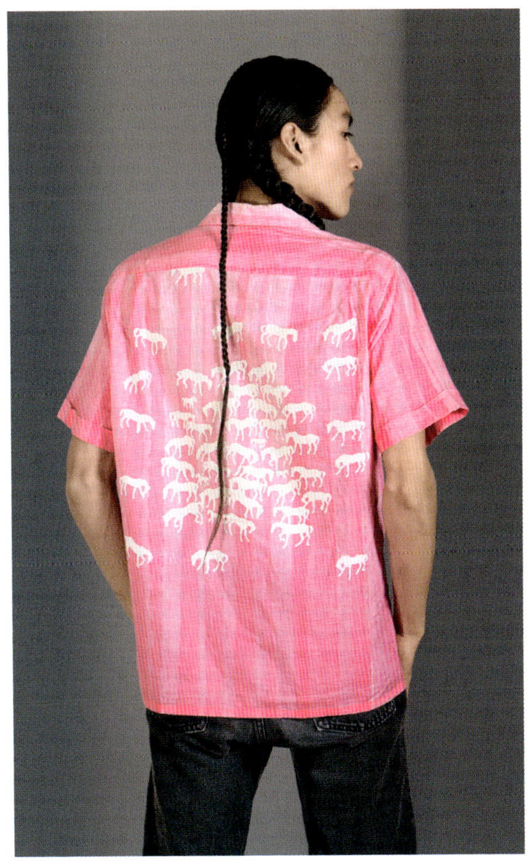

Phillip modeling shirt on facing page. Photo by Kitty Leaken.

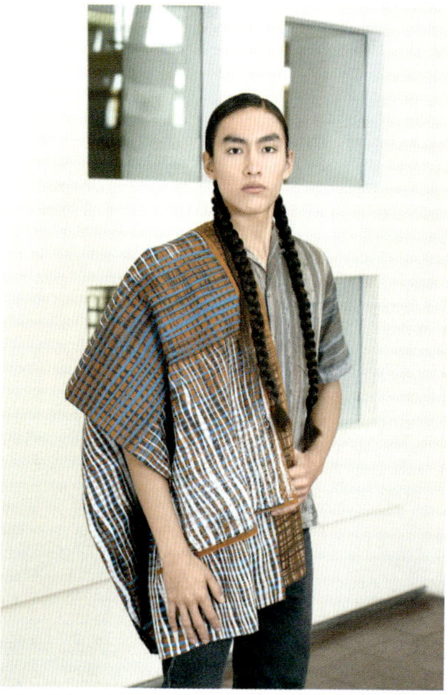

Phillip displaying Lloyd Kiva New designed textile of irregular plaid.
Courtesy of Aysen New Collection. Photo by Kitty Leaken.

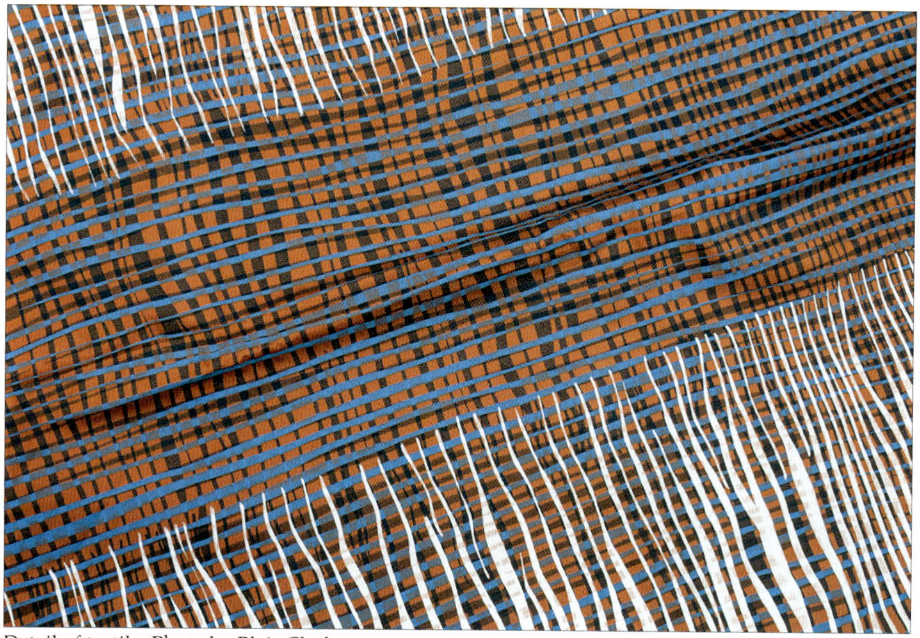

Detail of textile. Photo by Blair Clark.

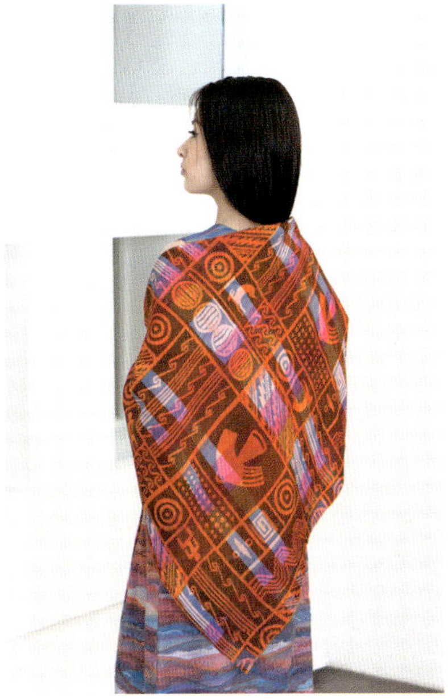

Wakeah displaying Lloyd Kiva New designed textile with pottery motifs.
Courtesy of Aysen New Collection. Photo by Kitty Leaken.

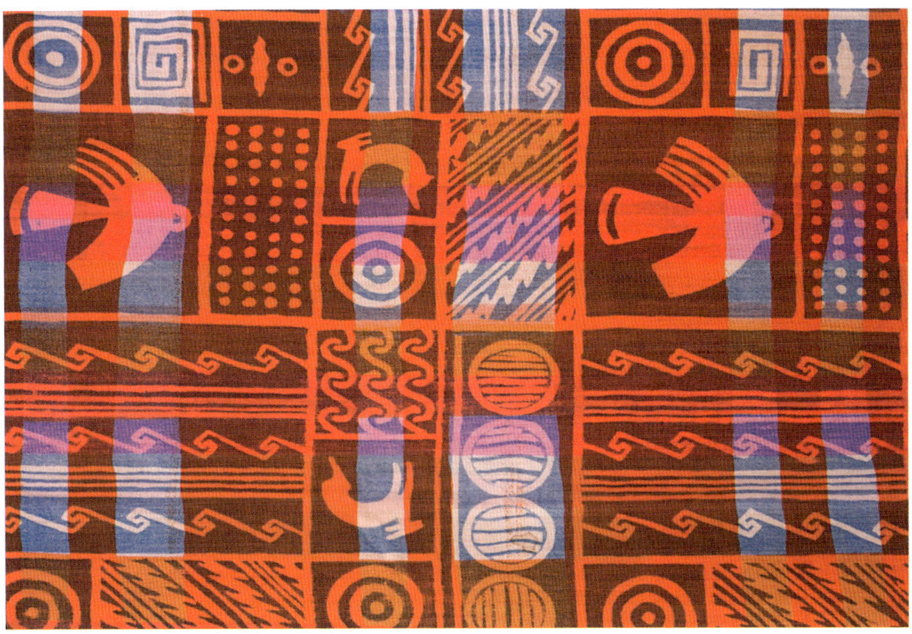

Detail of textile. Photo by Blair Clark.

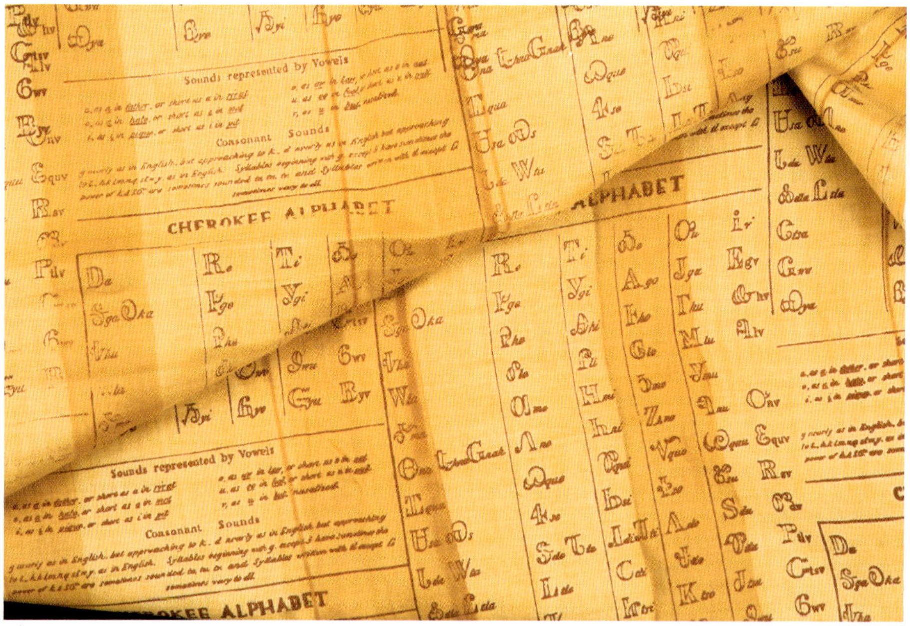

Cherokee Syllabary textile, detail. Courtesy of Aysen New Collection. Photo by Blair Clark.

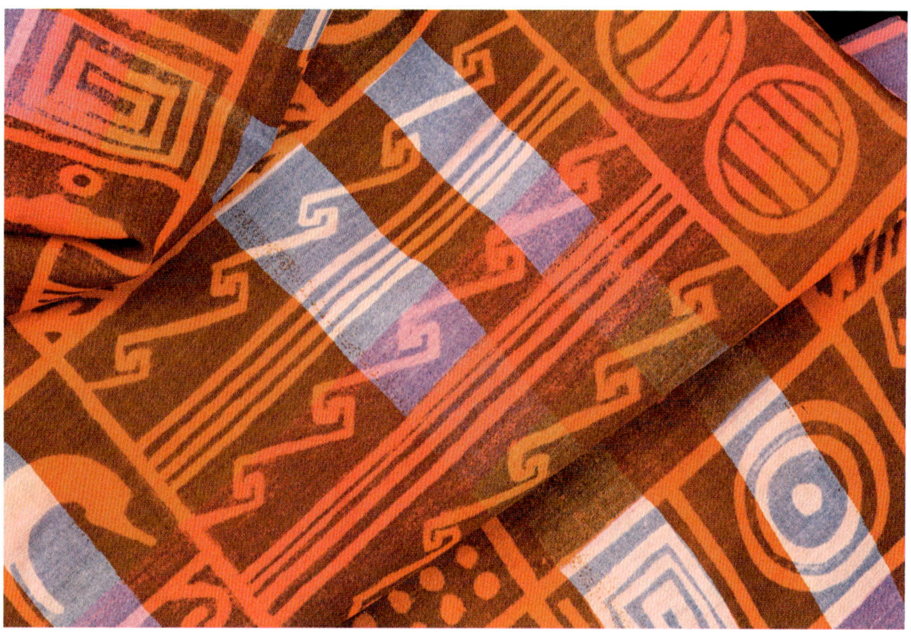

Pottery motif textile, detail. Courtesy of Aysen New Collection. Photo by Blair Clark.

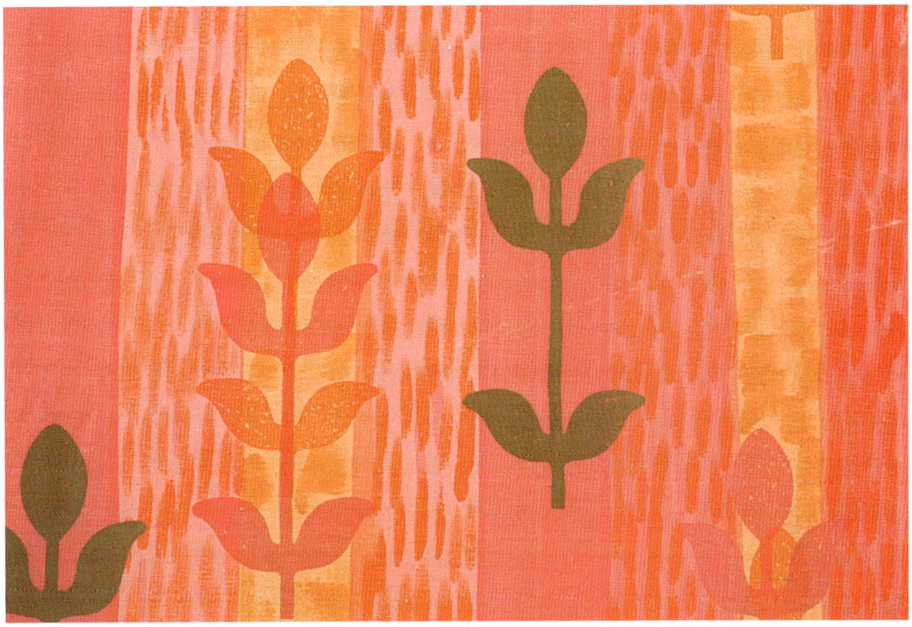

Plant motif textile, detail. Courtesy of Aysen New Collection. Photo by Blair Clark.

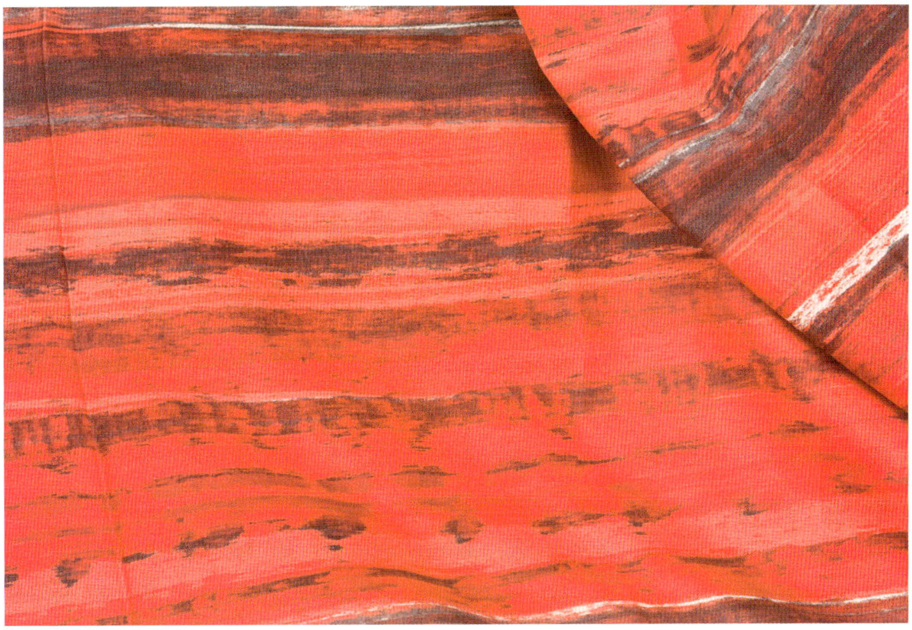

Red bands textile, detail. Courtesy of Aysen New Collection. Photo by Blair Clark.

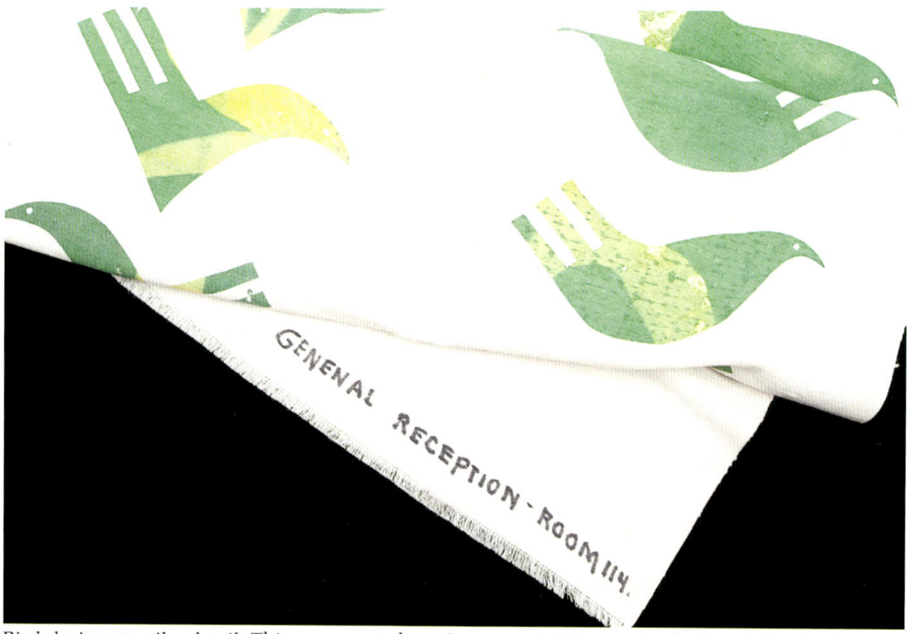

Bird designs textile, detail. This appears to have been created for use in the hospitality industry. Courtesy of Aysen New Collection. Photo by Blair Clark.

Lloyd Kiva New: Art, Design, and Influence

Lloyd Kiva New: Art, Design, and Influence was team-curated by Ryan S. Flahive, IAIA Archivist; Rose Marie Cutropia, Independent Curator; and Tatiana Lomahaftewa-Singer, (Hopi-Choctow) Curator of Collections, IAIA Museum of Contemporary Native Arts.

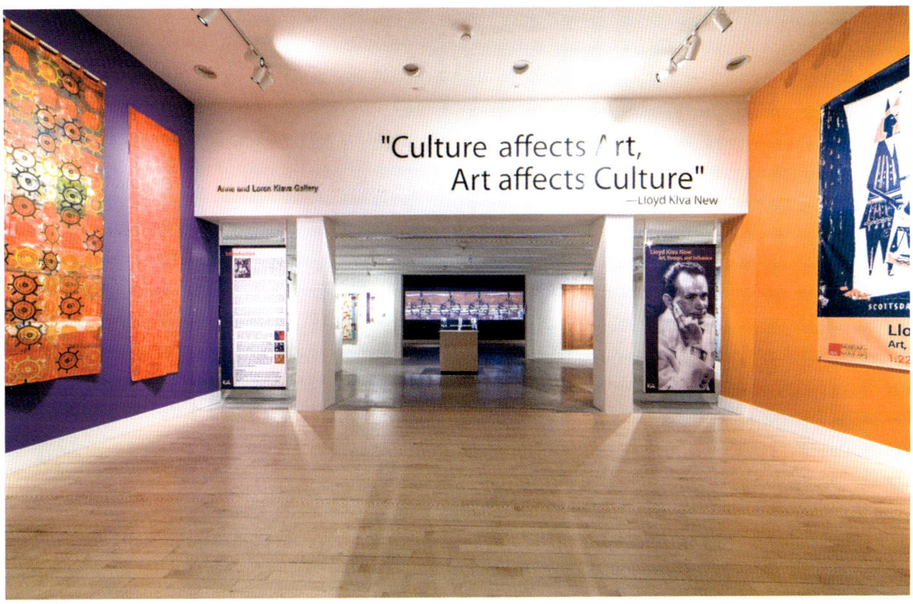

IAIA Museum of Contemporary Native Arts Foyer looking into Main Gallery. Photo by Jason S. Ordaz.

Lloyd Kiva New: Art, Design, and Influence draws upon three major elements of the career of Lloyd Henri "Kiva" New: artistic vision, design prowess, and his influence upon generations of Native artists. Each component is tied to his innovative concepts in Native art and culturally-based art education and is a testimony to his impact on the world of contemporary Native art.

Lloyd Kiva New: Art

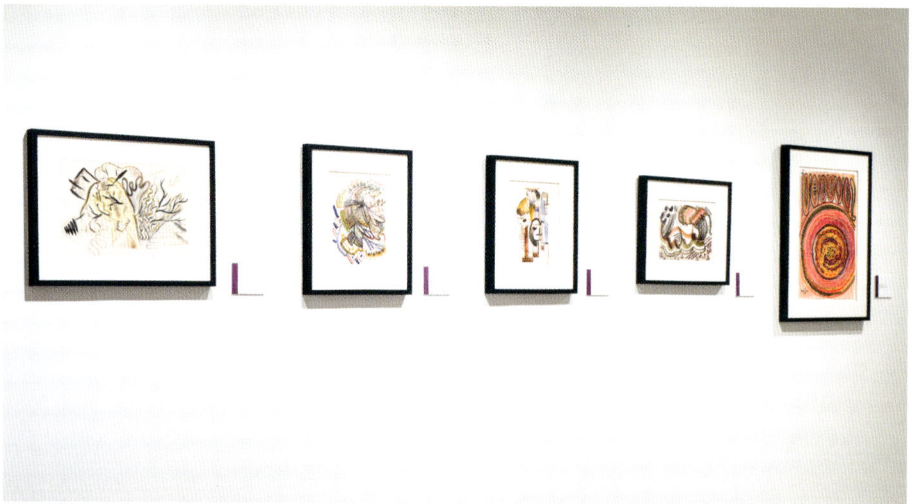

IAIA Museum of Contemporary Native Arts North Gallery. Photo by Jason S. Ordaz.

Until recently, Lloyd Kiva New's paintings remained in his personal archives in his Santa Fe home. New's widow Aysen New, longtime champion of his legacy, provided access to hundreds of his paintings, sketches, and drawings for *Lloyd Kiva New: Art*. The artworks are reflections of an artist who enjoyed painting for himself, without thought of an audience.

Lloyd Kiva New understood at an early age that he wanted to be an artist. By age six, New taught himself to grind and mix pigments extracted from an exposed coal vein and experimented with accessible binders like machinery oil. In high school, New received enough recognition for his artistic talents to pursue an art career "but was embarrassed to let that be known, for I feared I would lose family and community support. Artists were viewed as strange people who wore berets, were immoral, and eventually starved to death…"[1]

A trip to Chicago in 1933 changed the course of New's life. He visited the Museum of the Art Institute of Chicago, where he would

1 Lloyd Kiva New, *The Sound of Drums: A Memoir of Lloyd Kiva New*. Ed. Ryan S. Flahive. (Santa Fe: Sunstone Press, 2016), 118.

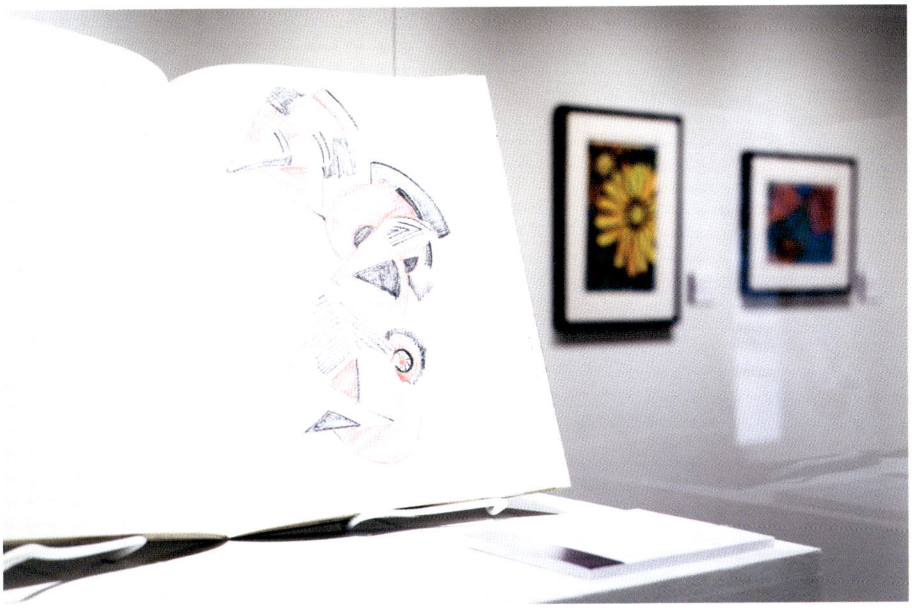

Lloyd Kiva New (Cherokee), Sketchbook, c. 1938, in the IAIA Museum of Contemporary Native Arts North Gallery. Photo by Jason S. Ordaz.

return to school and earn a degree in Art Education in 1938. New was inspired by the Pre-Columbian collection at the Art Institute, "I was astounded by the great cities of the Aztecs, the works in gold and silver, the murals of Bonampak, the ceramic arts, and the textiles of Peru. These were my people."[2]

New moved to Phoenix in 1939 to teach art at the Phoenix Indian Boarding School and encountered a desert landscape that influenced his art and design throughout his career. During his short time at the school, New accompanied Hopi artist Charles Loloma to the 1939 Golden Gate International Exposition in San Francisco, where murals were painted in the Social Realism genre of the 1930s, a style that remained with New during much of his life and can be seen in his paintings.

In 1941, Lloyd H. New enlisted in the United States Navy. As Lieutenant and Deck Officer, New served as an official artist for the USS Sanborn (APA 193). New's role as the ship artist was extensive: he

2 Ibid., 128.

designed the boat's seal and installed a painted mural aboard the ship. While aboard the ship from 1941-1945, the Sanborn traveled from port to port and New painted or sketched what he saw: Tulagi, the Marshall Islands, New Caledonia, Maui, Honolulu, Guam, and Saipan to name a few. These images remain the memory of the Sanborn's war journey.

On February 18, 1945, the Sanborn moved troops to and from the island of Iwo Jima, where a decisive battle was fought against Japanese forces. New's first person imagery of the Battle of Iwo Jima and perspective from aboard a landing craft provide life and color to a story primarily documented through black and white photographs and newsreels. "For six days and nights the crews aboard my twelve landing craft transported wounded and dead back to the outlying hospital ships."[3] Lloyd New's wartime watercolor paintings are cherished as works of art and part of the historical record.

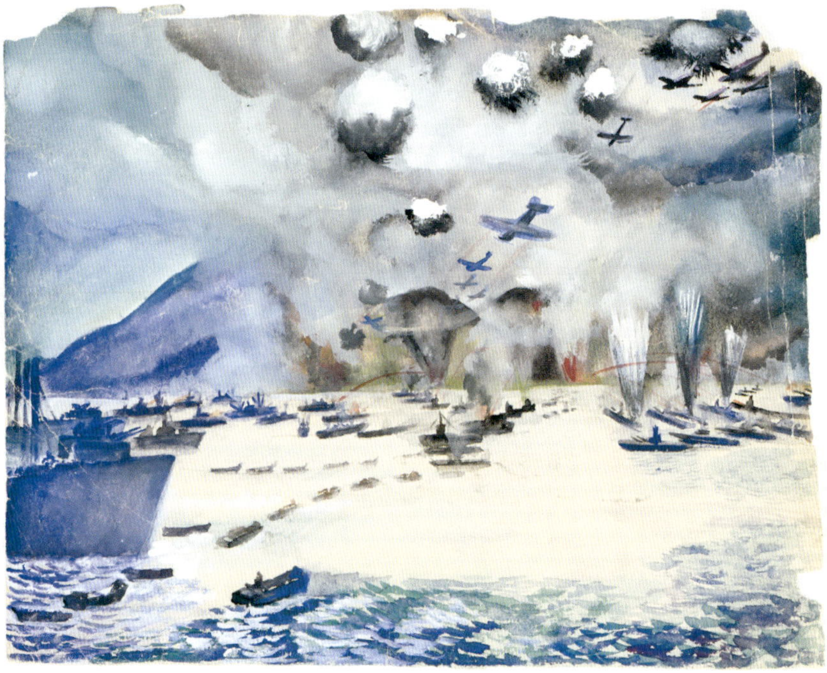

Lloyd Kiva New (Cherokee), *Battle of Iwo Jima,* watercolor on paper, 8.5 x 11 in., 1945. Courtesy of Aysen New Collection. Photo by Jason S. Ordaz.

3 Ibid., 140.

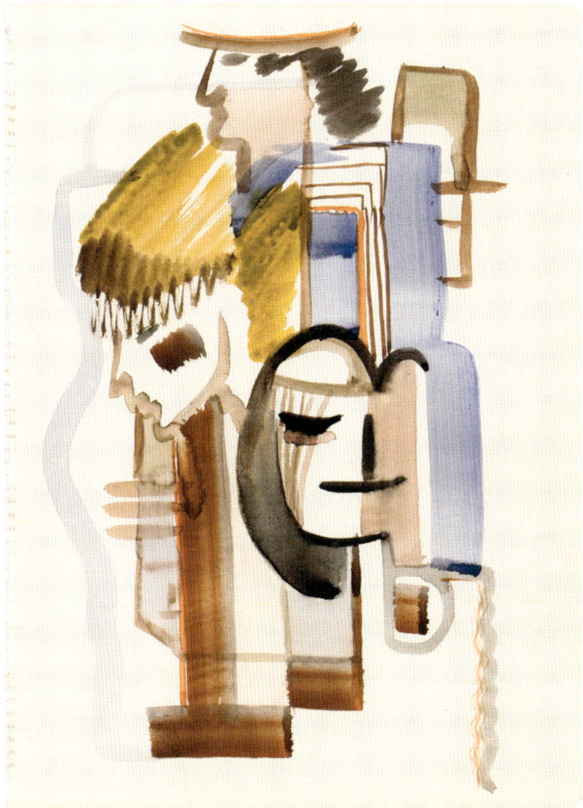

Lloyd Kiva New (Cherokee), Untitled, watercolor on paper, 11.75 x 9 in., 1941. Courtesy of IAIA Archives, Santa Fe, NM. Photo by Jason S. Ordaz.

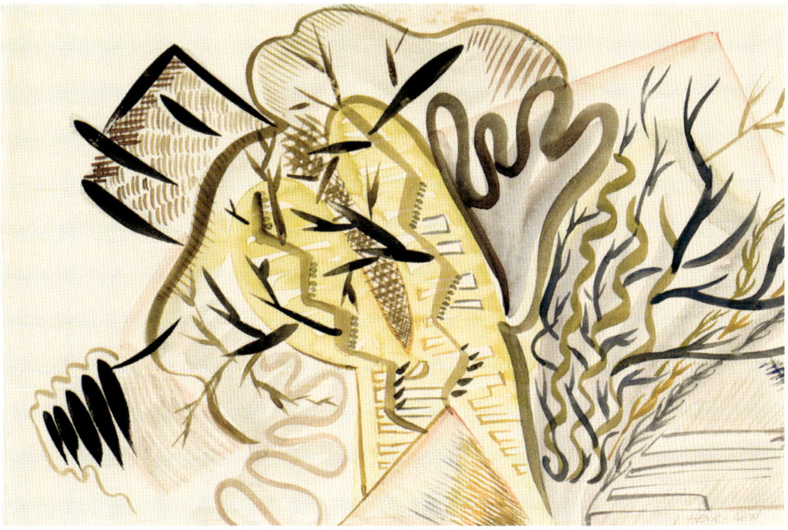

Lloyd Kiva New (Cherokee), Untitled, watercolor on paper, 11.5 x 17 in., 1941. Courtesy of IAIA Archives, Santa Fe, NM. Photo by Jason S. Ordaz.

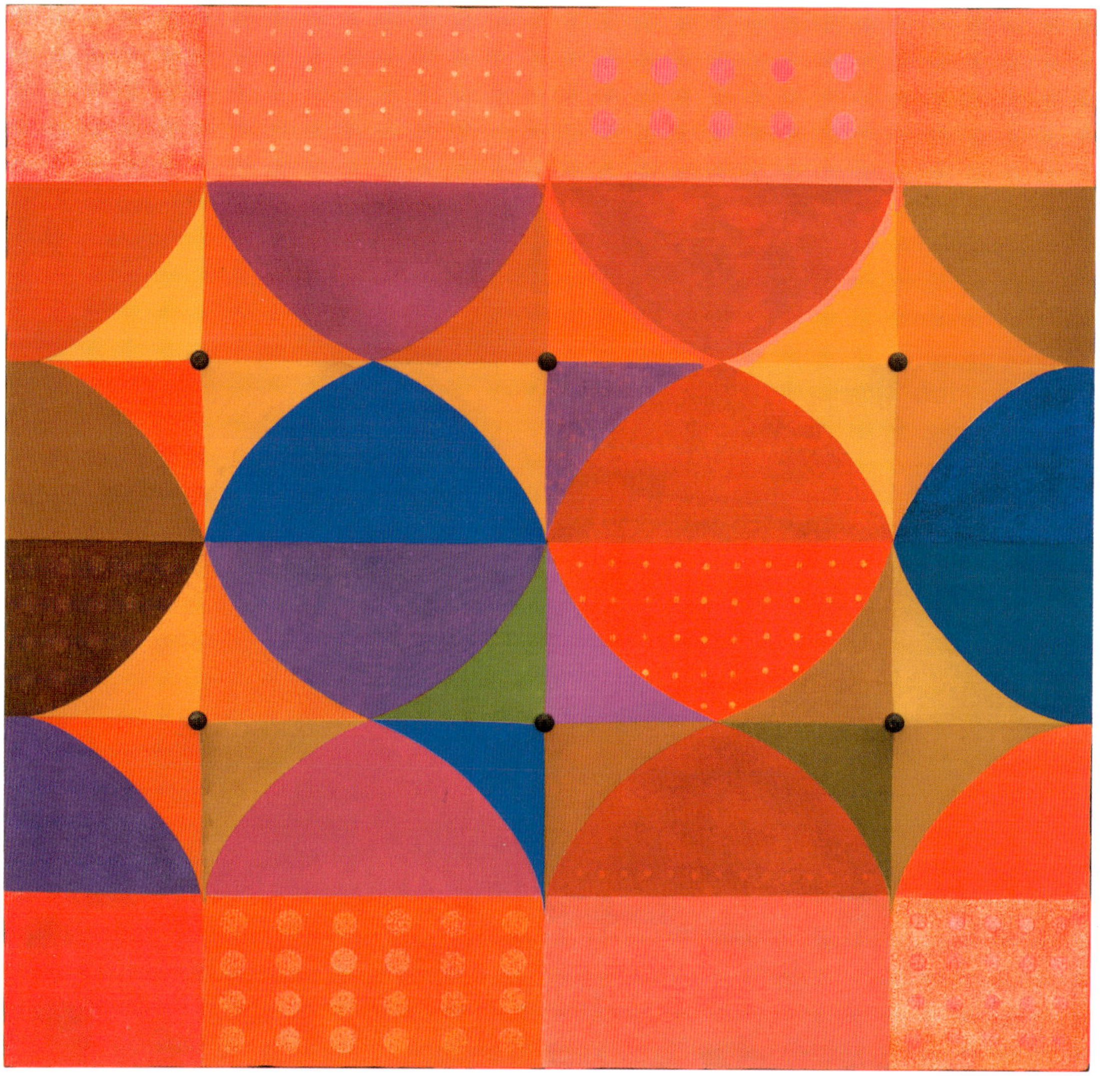

Lloyd Kiva New (Cherokee), *Indian Beadwork,* oil and metal studs on canvas, 51 x 48.125 in., 1973. Courtesy of IAIA Museum of Contemporary Native Arts, Santa Fe, NM: Che-121. Photo by Jason S. Ordaz.

Lloyd Kiva New: Design

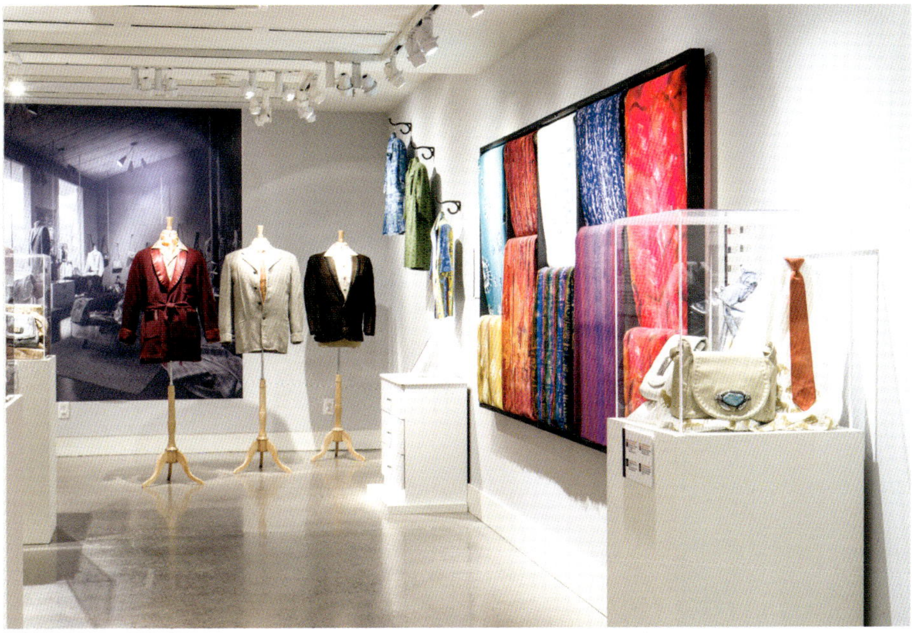

IAIA Museum of Contemporary Native Arts, Fritz Scholder Gallery. Photo by Jason S. Ordaz.

Upon returning to Arizona after World War II, Lloyd Kiva New ventured into fashion design through an invitation to join a group of like-minded artists in Scottsdale, a collective known today as the Arizona Designer Craftsmen. Around 1947, The Arizona Craftsmen Center opened on the corner of Main Street and Brown Avenue where New developed the Lloyd Kiva brand and set in motion a new design trend that fused Native elements with modern fashion. New's goal was to "convert the image of Indian art in economic terms from the beaded rabbit's foot level to something that was dignified and serious; I wanted to see if young, contemporary-minded Indian people could do worthy contemporary things."[4]

Utilizing his love of leather, traditionally woven textiles, and hand-dyed fabrics, New expressed his artistic freedom though a line of "Kiva

4 Lloyd Kiva New, interview by Sam Myers, October 7, 1975, *Listening to Indians* no. 57–58, transcript, St. Louis Community College-Florissant Valley, St Louis, MO, 7.

Bags," leather hats, dresses, men's shirts, and yards of printed fabrics. He employed a number of other Native American artists, including Manfred Susunkewa (Hopi), Charles Loloma (Hopi), Frank Austin Bahazhonie (Navajo), and Andrew Van Tsinhajinnie (Navajo) to develop a line of haute couture and ready-to-wear fashion.

In 1952, Lloyd Kiva attended the International Fashion Show in Atlantic City and met Leslie Tillett, a well-known fashion designer and textile artist. New studied with Tillett in the following months and learned how to produce his own hand-dyed fabrics on a large-scale. Upon his return to Scottsdale, New entered into a limited wholesale textile business that featured hand-screened fabrics of distinctive Native designs, which became a hallmark of the Lloyd Kiva style.

A unique feature of the Lloyd Kiva aesthetic was "color clash," a combination of off-tone colors underneath the designs. The "color clash" aesthetic was reminiscent of the sky and the mountains with earth tone

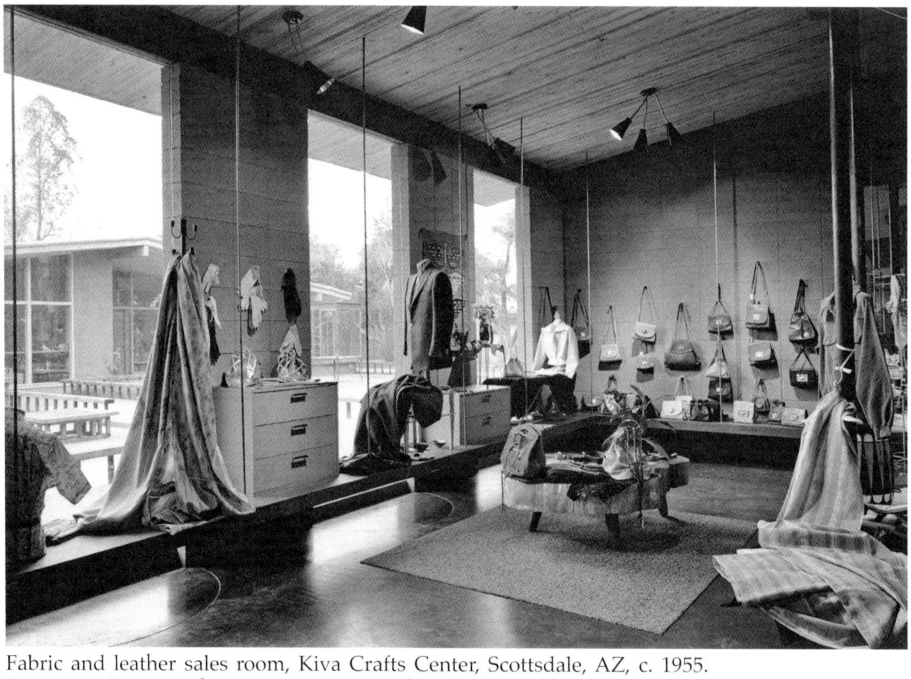

Fabric and leather sales room, Kiva Crafts Center, Scottsdale, AZ, c. 1955. Courtesy of IAIA Archives, Santa Fe, NM. Photo by Stuart Weiner.

reds, greyed-out blues, and desert purples, "If you see them together in nature, then they are beautiful," New said in a 1961 interview.[5] New's printed textiles established the artistic and design aesthetic later incorporated into student textiles at the Institute of American Indian Arts (IAIA).

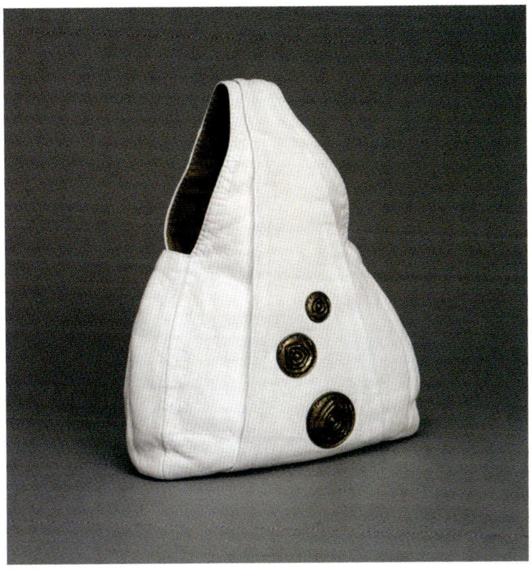

Lloyd Kiva New (Cherokee), handbag, white leather with metal medallion by Charles Loloma (Hopi), c. 1950. Courtesy of Doreen Picerne and *Fashion by Robert Black*. Photo by Jason S. Ordaz.

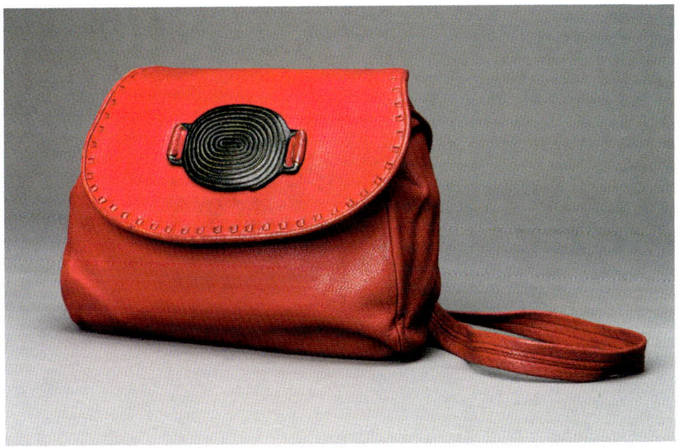

Lloyd Kiva New (Cherokee), handbag, rose-colored leather with metal medallion by Charles Loloma (Hopi), c. 1950. Courtesy of Doreen Picerne and *Fashion by Robert Black*. Photo by Jason S. Ordaz.

5 "Designers Set Fashion Mood," *The Arizona Republic*, (Phoenix, AZ), January 29, 1961.

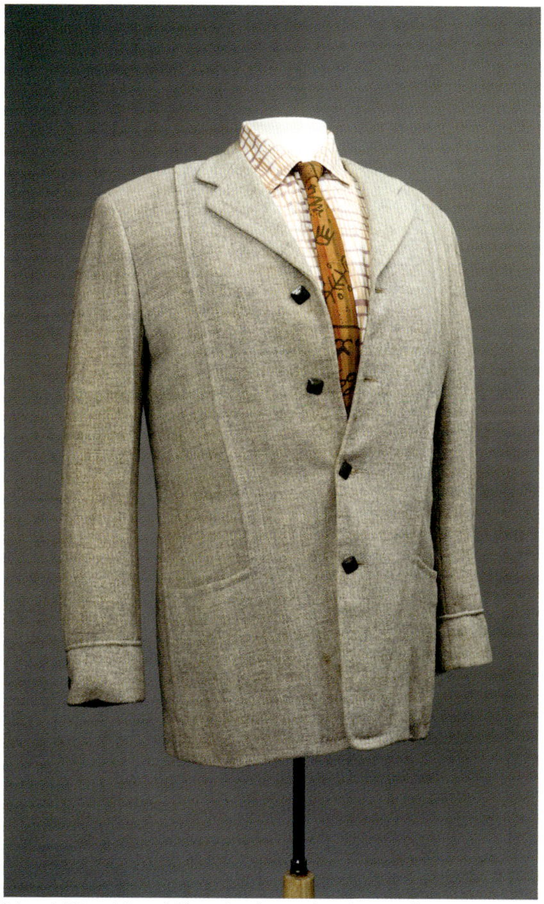

Lloyd Kiva New (Cherokee), wool jacket with metal buttons by Charles Loloma (Hopi), cotton shirt and silk tie, c. 1950. Shirt and tie courtesy of Aysen New. Jacket courtesy of IAIA Museum of Contemporary Native Arts, Santa Fe, NM: Che-114. Photo by Jason S. Ordaz.

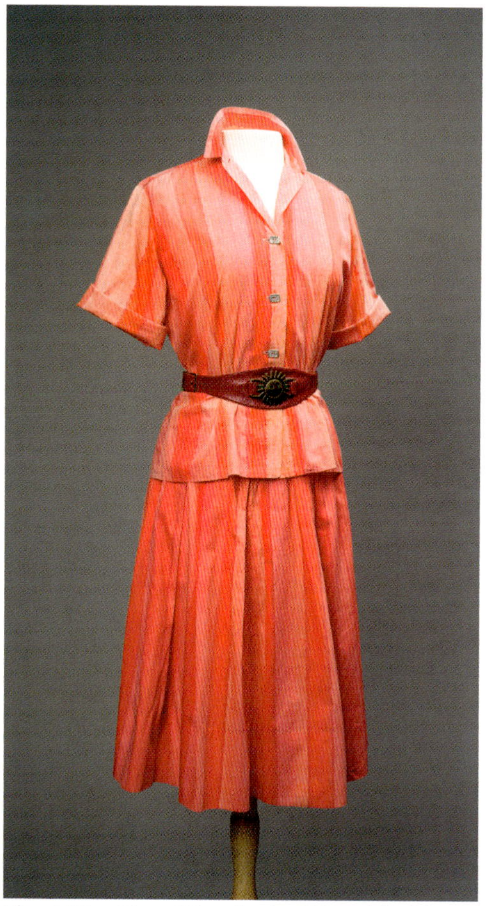

Lloyd Kiva New (Cherokee), cotton skirt/blouse, fabric dyes with leather belt, c. 1950. Courtesy of Aysen New. Photo by Jason S. Ordaz.

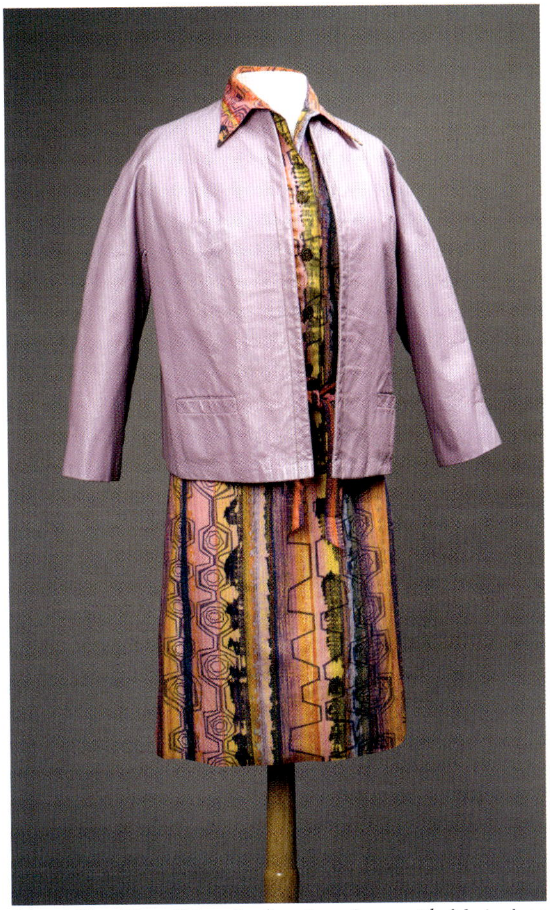

Lloyd Kiva New (Cherokee), cotton dress with fabric dyes with leather jacket, c. 1950. Courtesy of Dorren Picerne and *Fashion by Robert Black.* Photo by Jason S. Ordaz.

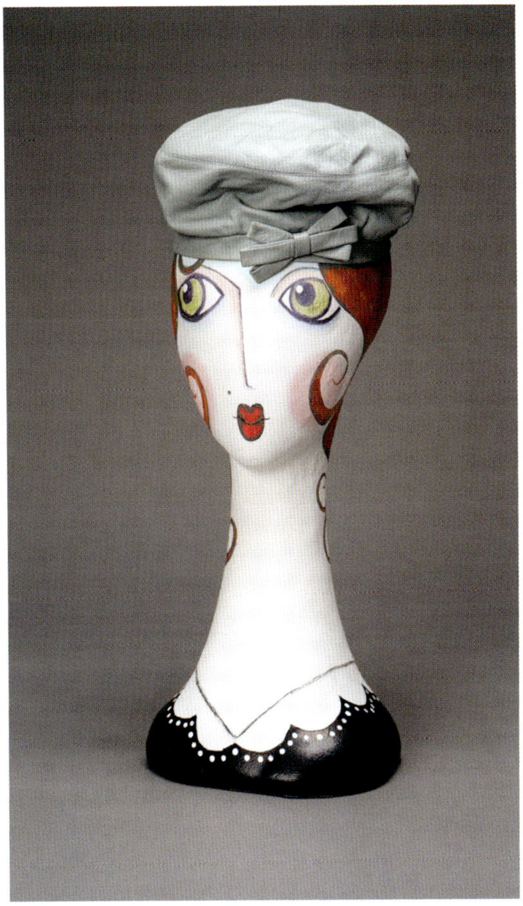

Lloyd Kiva New (Cherokee), leather hat, c. 1950. Courtesy of Dorren Picerne and *Fashion by Robert Black.* Photo by Jason S. Ordaz.

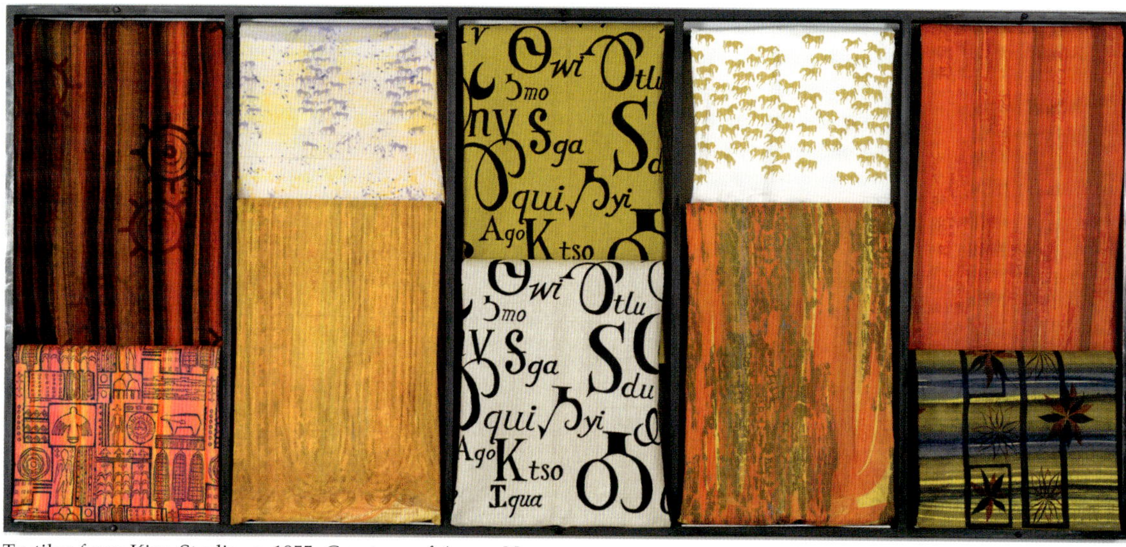

Textiles from Kiva Studio, c. 1955. Courtesy of Aysen New Collection. Photo by Jason S. Ordaz.

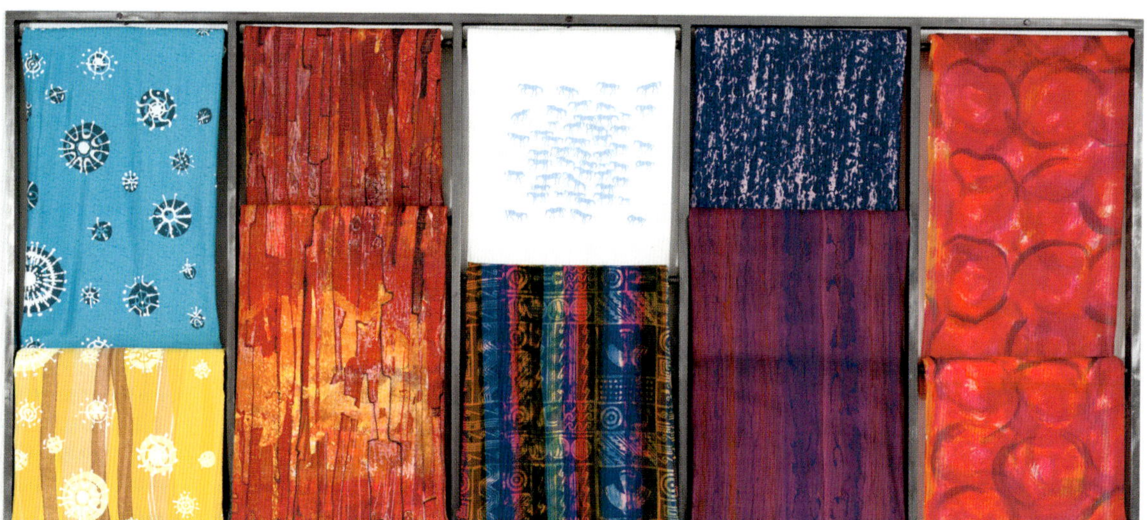

Textiles from Kiva Studio, c. 1955. Courtesy of Aysen New Collection. Photo by Jason S. Ordaz.

Lloyd Kiva New: Influence

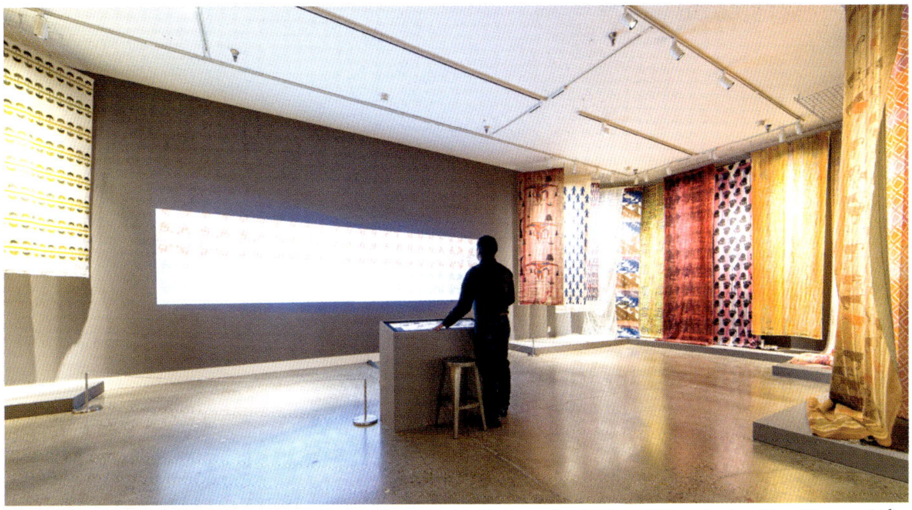

IAIA Museum of Contemporary Native Arts Main Gallery featuring IAIA student textiles and the Lloyd Kiva New Design Station Interactive. Photo by Jason S. Ordaz.

By the late 1950s, New returned to art education. Building upon his prior teaching experience, New shaped his philosophic approach towards Native arts and crafts production and, in 1959, was invited to co-direct the Southwest Indian Arts and Crafts Workshop at the University of Arizona in Tucson. Supported by the Rockefeller Foundation, the workshop was based upon New's educational theories and concepts: "the future of Indian art lies in the future, not the past… Let's be more concerned with the evolution of artists rather than art products. Let's see that the young Indian realizes the values of his great and wonderful traditions as the springboard for his own personal creative ideas."[6] New believed that the concept of culture was vital for human learning. Art could be used as a source of personal creative expression and the basis for finding one's identity in a world of constant change and transition. The Workshop was a success and New's pedagogical concepts became the basis for a new art school in

6 University of Arizona, "A Proposal for an Exploratory Workshop for Talented Younger Indians," October 15, 1959. Lloyd H. New Papers, IAIA Archives, Santa Fe, New Mexico.

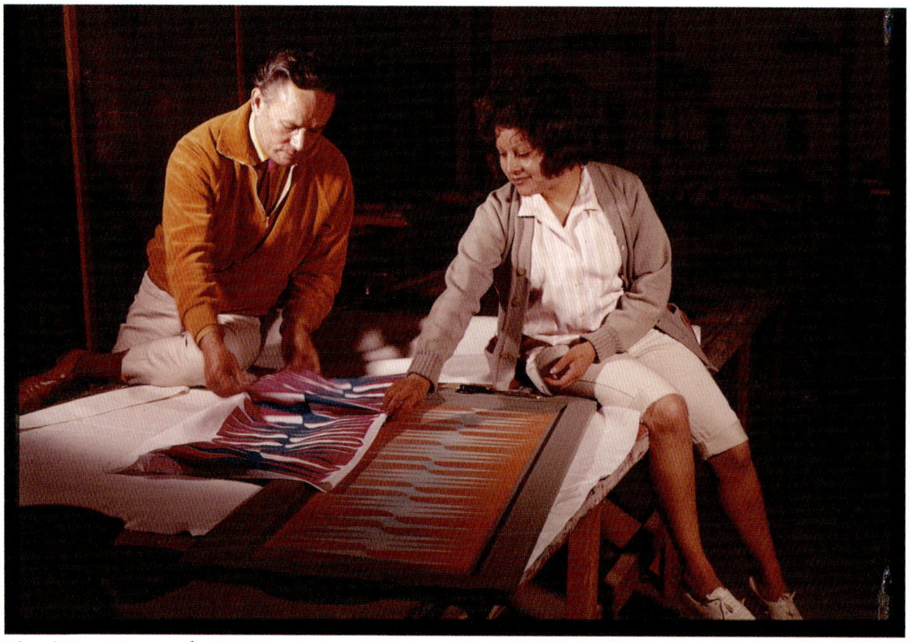

Lloyd Kiva New with IAIA Student, c. 1963. Courtesy of IAIA Archives, Santa Fe, NM. Photo by Kay V. Wiest.

the Bureau of Indian Affairs (BIA) system—the Institute of American Indian Arts in Santa Fe, New Mexico, that opened in October of 1962.

IAIA's founding philosophy was that unique cultural traditions were to be honored and used creatively and lead to a "meaningful and productive contemporary life."[7] The school was a government funded education experiment and at the helm of its arts program was Lloyd Kiva New. Hired as the first Art Director of IAIA, Lloyd Kiva New implemented innovative theories on learning and creativity that changed the landscape of Native American art.

New taught IAIA students the textile design process used in his Scottsdale-based Kiva Studio through a formal printed textile course. Vibrant colors, creative arrangements, and use of Native design elements in student work is evidence of Lloyd New's influence on IAIA students. New recognized his students carried an inherent sense of design that could be drawn out through contemporary printing

7 Lloyd H. New, "The Role of the Institute of American Indian Arts in the Development of Indian Education and its Potential as a Major Cultural Institution," Feb 1969, 3, Lloyd H. New Papers, IAIA Archives, Santa Fe, New Mexico.

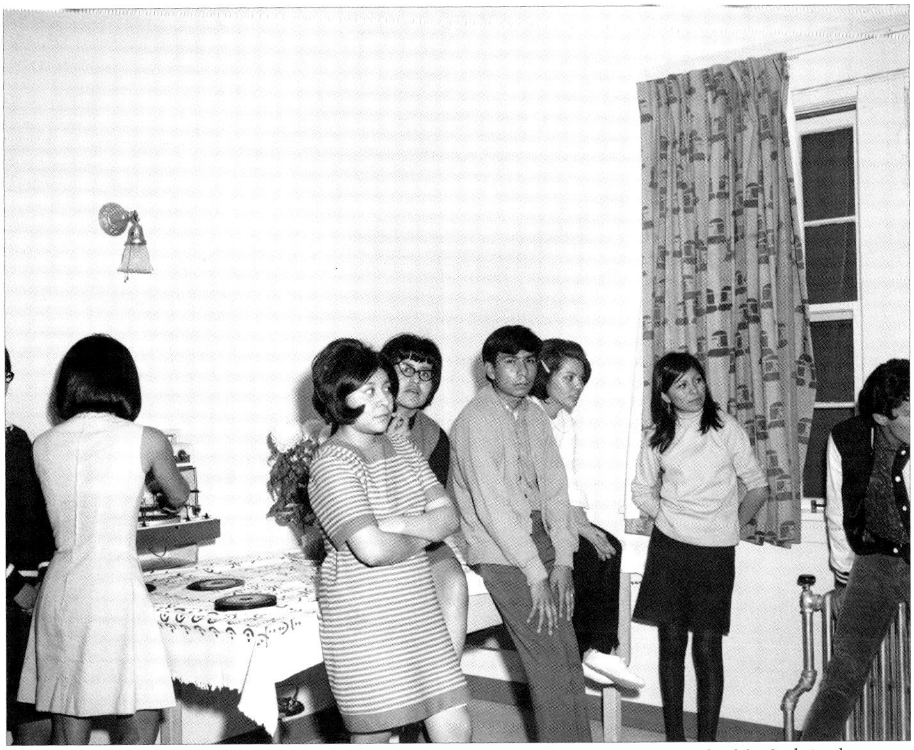

IAIA students on campus with printed textiles used as window coverings and tablecloth in the background, c. 1966. Courtesy of IAIA Archives, Santa Fe, NM.

techniques. New encouraged his textile students to experiment with color, texture, design, and layering. The student artists created designs on large screens up to four feet wide, which gave them the ability to screen on pieces of cotton, burlap, linen, or canvas as long as thirty feet or more. The result of New's work with students was an output of modern textiles using familiar cultural motifs in unconventional arrangements and colors. Nearly 200 student textiles are held in the permanent collection at the IAIA Museum of Contemporary Native Arts.

The printed textiles show student experimentation and the influence of modern design aesthetics on their work. Developed for practical applications, some of the textiles were made into curtains and draperies for IAIA dormitories, offices, and other buildings. Printed fabrics were also used as table coverings, wall hangings, and clothing. Although used in a pragmatic way, the student textiles were also seen as works of art and included in exhibits in the IAIA Gallery and later the IAIA Museum in the 1960s and 70s.

Lloyd Kiva New: Art, Design, and Influence is a tribute to a pioneer; a Cherokee artist and educator who saw past stereotypical notions of Native art and approached art as a vehicle to sustain culture in a changing world. In the words of Lloyd Kiva New, "Ultimately, it is not the making of pretty pictures or things that enables the Indian youngster to bank those elements of his Native psyche, to be drawn upon for the rest of his life; it is discovering how to use his personal creative power to create meaningful responses to the ever-changing realities of a modern world as a proud, well-rounded productive Indian person."[8]

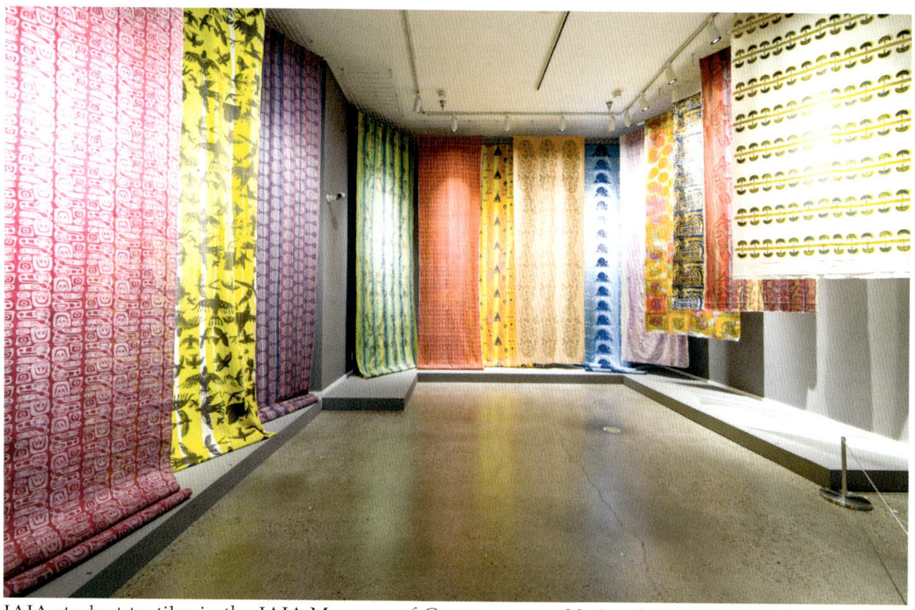

IAIA student textiles in the IAIA Museum of Contemporary Native Arts Main Gallery. Photo by Jason S. Ordaz.

8 *The Sound of Drums,* 180.

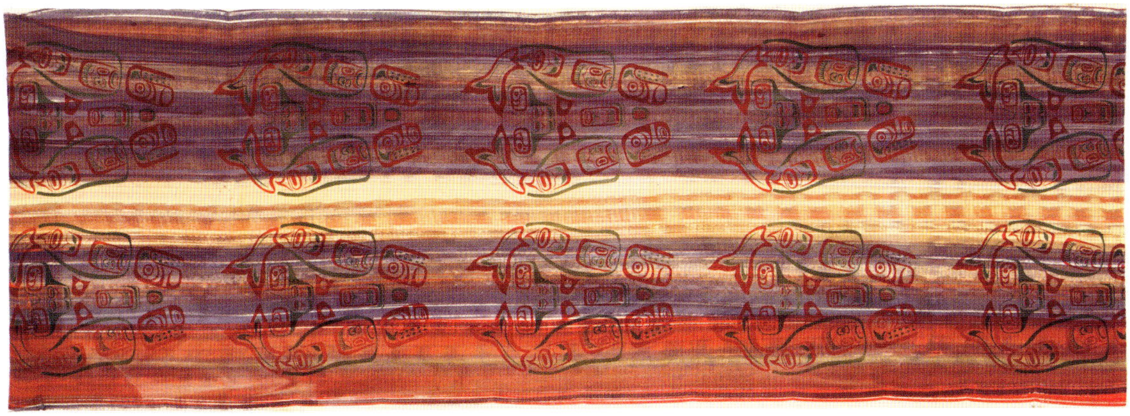

Unknown artist, textile, ink on cotton, 109.25 x 38.25 in., c. 1965. Courtesy of IAIA Museum of Contemporary Native Arts, Santa Fe, NM: Ath-26. Photo by Jason S. Ordaz.

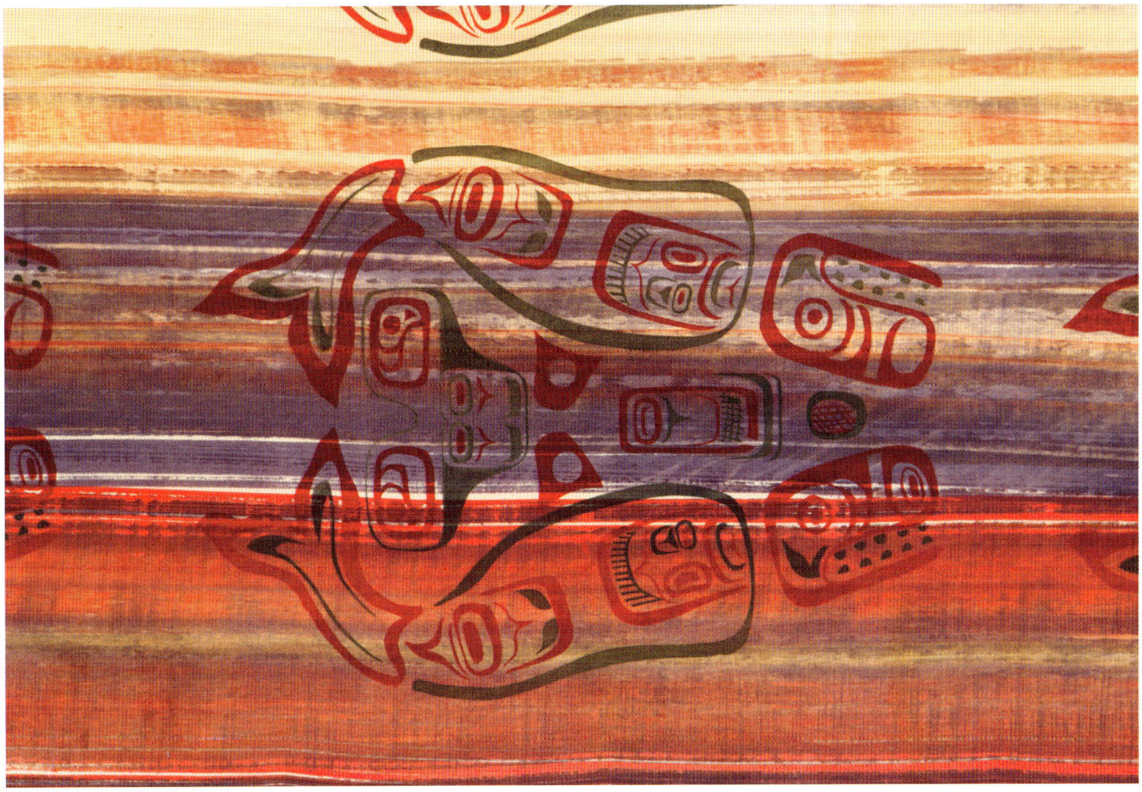

Detail.

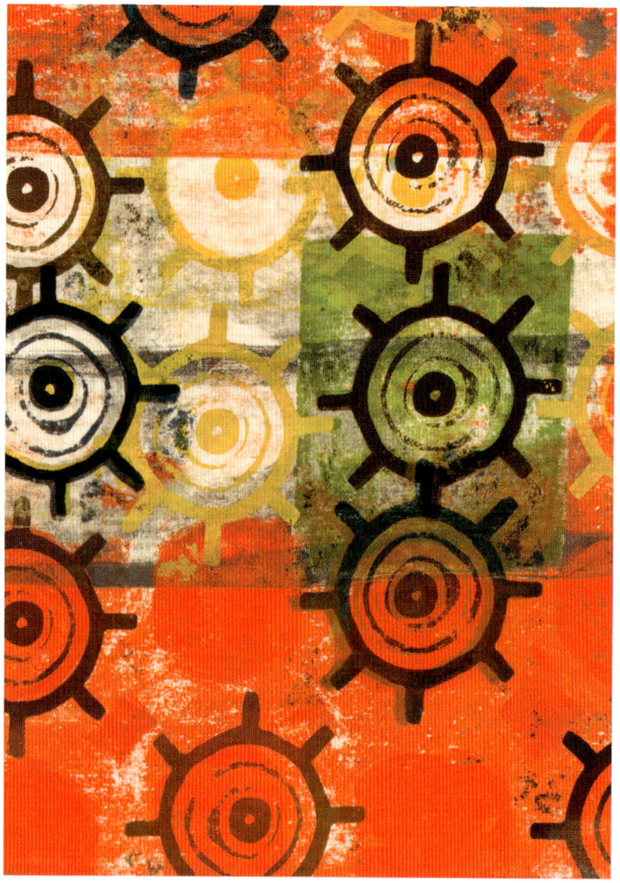

Detail.

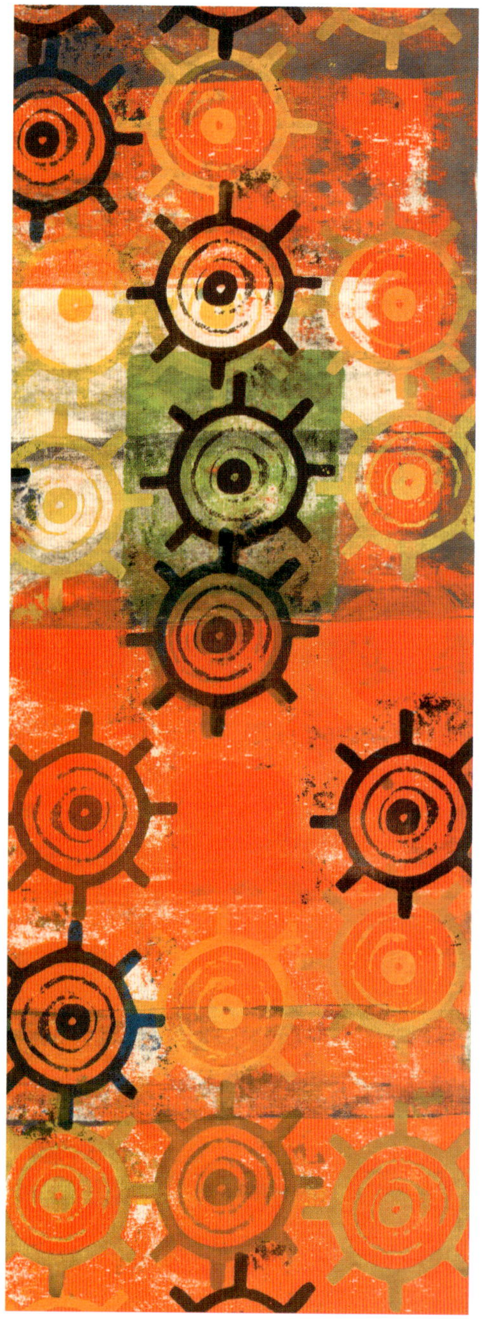

Lloyd Kiva New (Cherokee), textile, ink on cotton, 106.75 x 36.5 in., n.d. Courtesy of IAIA Museum of Contemporary Native Arts, Santa Fe, NM: Che-9. Photo by Jason S. Ordaz.

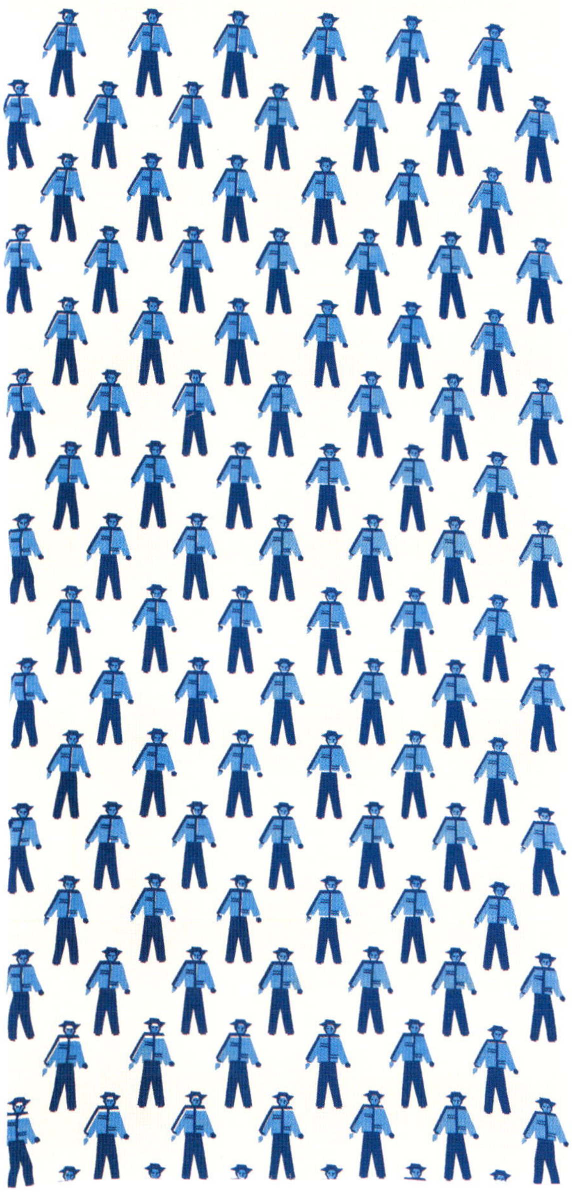

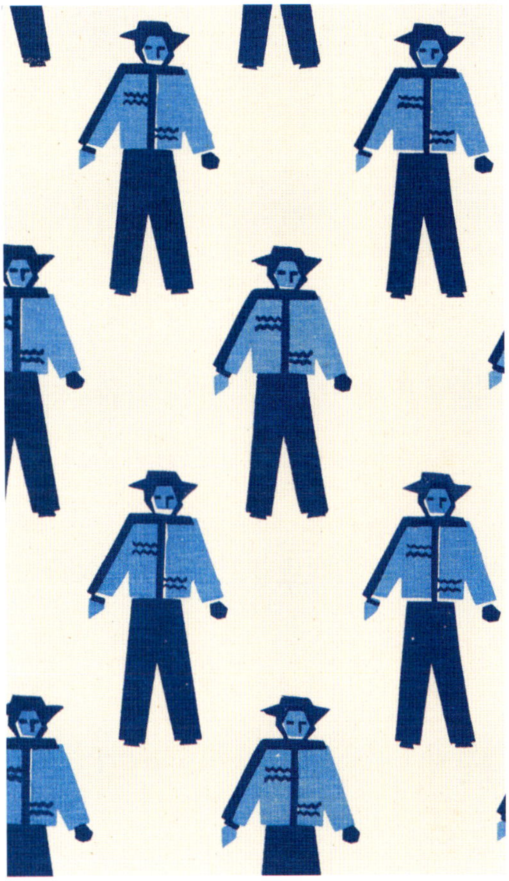

Detail.

Jennie Trujillo (Taos Pueblo), textile, ink on linen, 106 x 52 in., c. 1963. Courtesy of IAIA Museum of Contemporary Native Arts, Santa Fe, NM: Prop-496. Photo by Jason S. Ordaz.

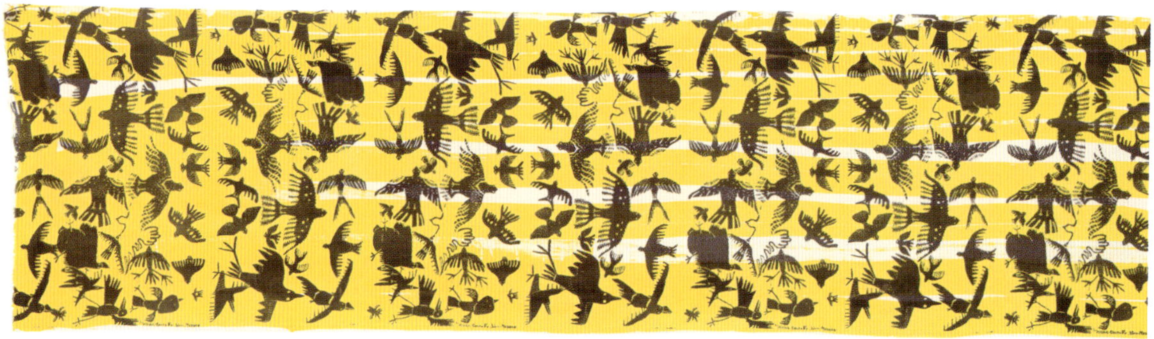

Carol Frazier Aikens (Paiute), textile, aniline dyes on cotton, 175 x 45.5 in., 1976. Courtesy of IAIA Museum of Contemporary Native Arts, Santa Fe, NM: Pu-38. Photo by Jason S. Ordaz.

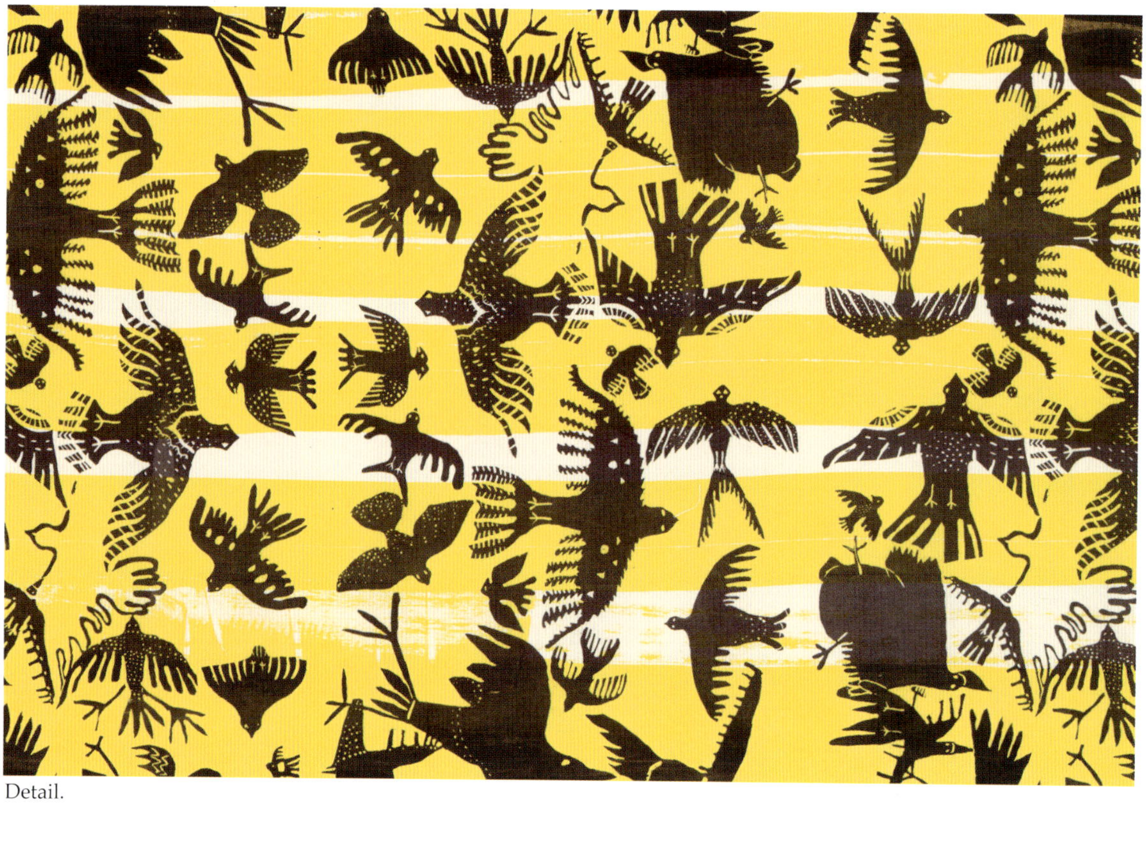

Detail.

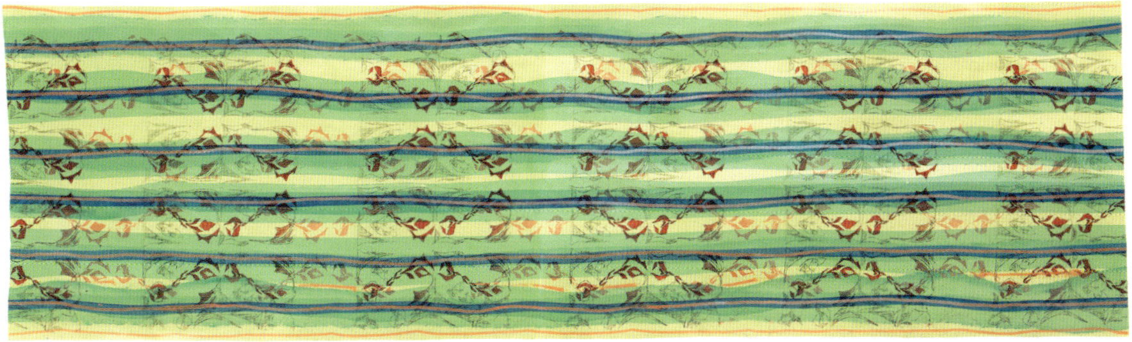

Unknown artist (possibly Carol Frazier Aikens, Paiute), textile, ink, and dyes on cotton, 148 x 47 in., 1976. Courtesy of IAIA Museum of Contemporary Native Arts, Santa Fe, NM: Pu-62. Photo by Jason S. Ordaz.

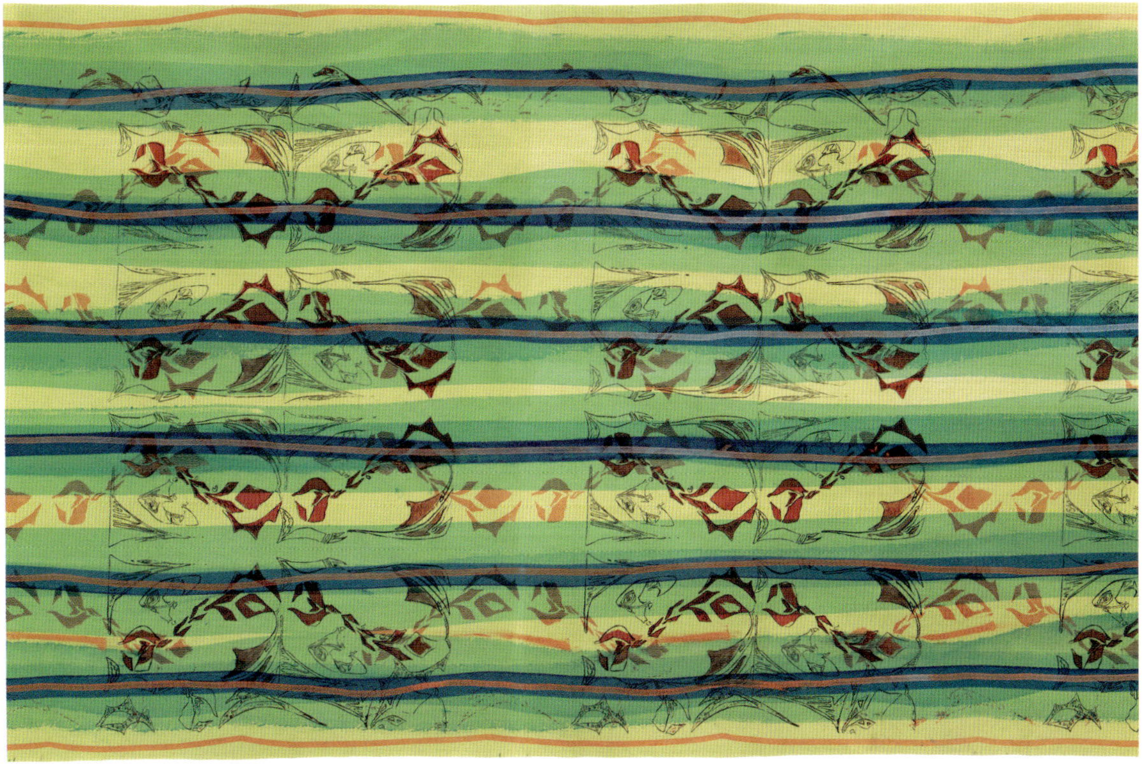

Detail.

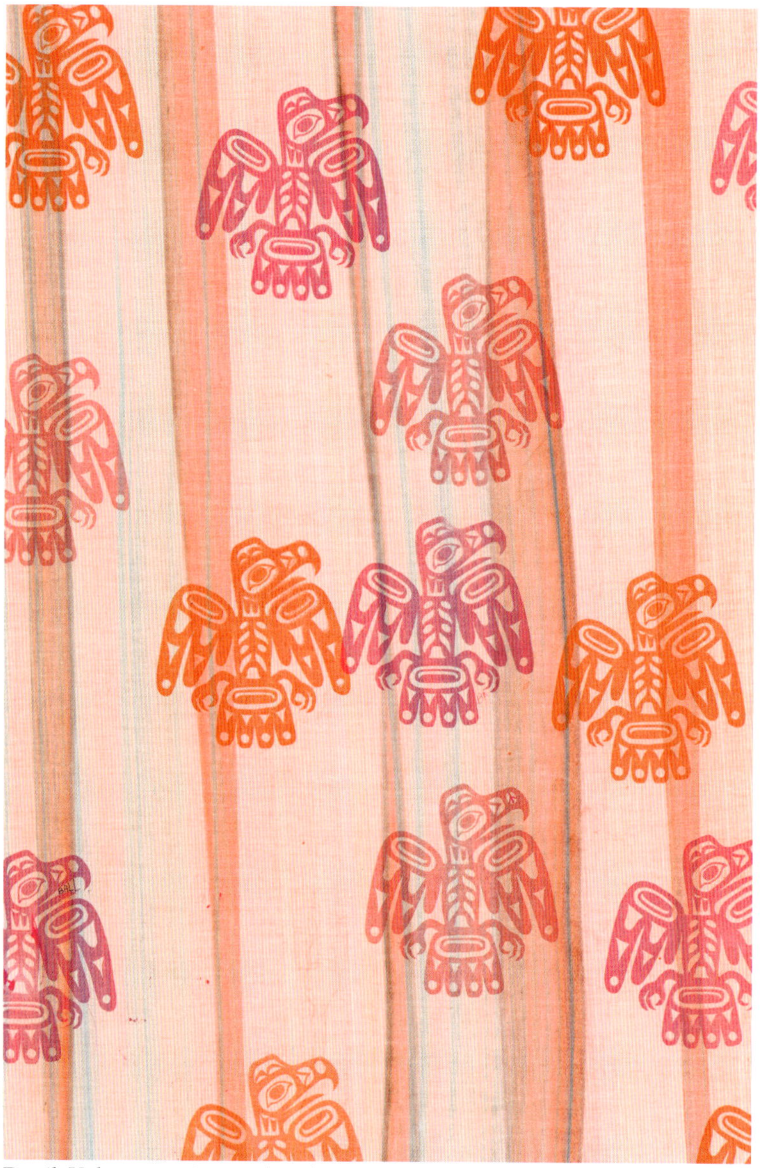

Detail. Unknown artist, textile, ink on cotton, 57 x 27 in., n.d. Courtesy of IAIA Museum of Contemporary Native Arts, Santa Fe, NM: Prop-3. Photo by Jason S. Ordaz.

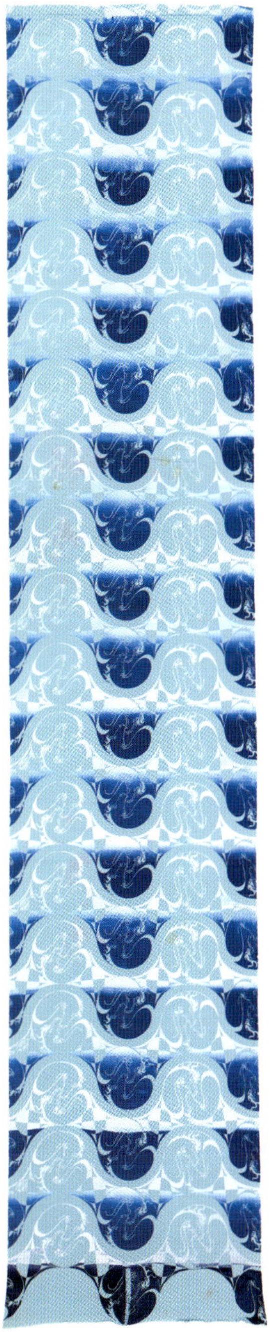

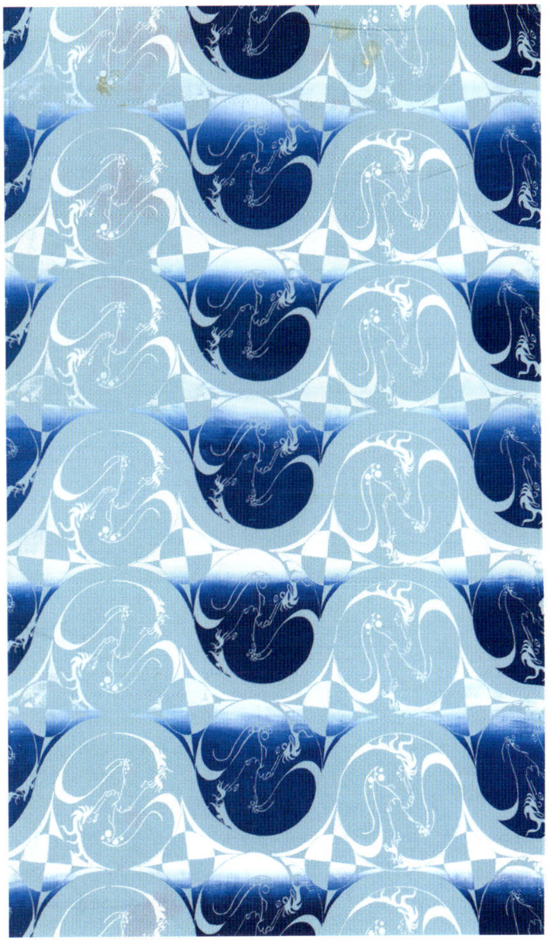

Detail.

Harrison Burnside (Navajo), textile, ink on cotton, 177 x 35.5 in., c. 1979. Courtesy of IAIA Museum of Contemporary Native Arts, Santa Fe, NM: N-149. Photo by Jason S. Ordaz.

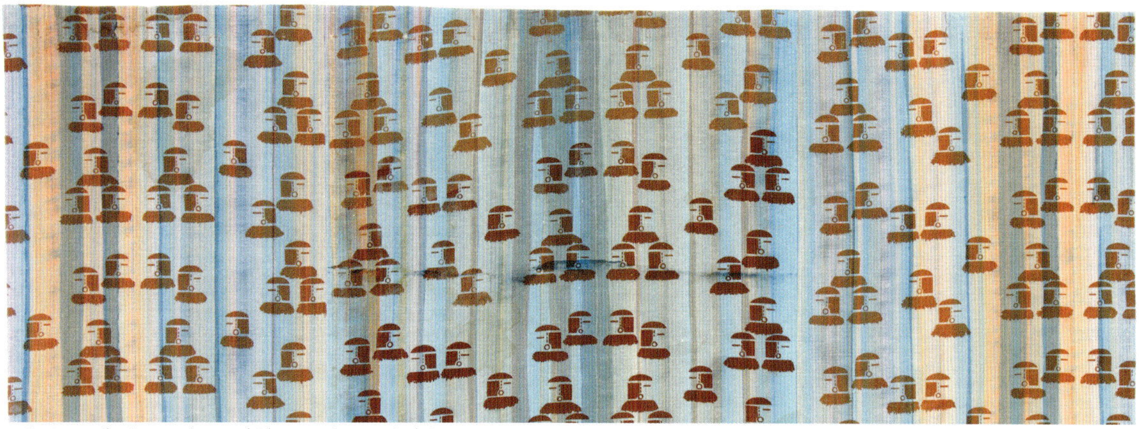

Linda Lomahaftewa (Hopi/Choctaw), textile/drapery, ink on cotton, 118 x 72.5 in., 1964. Courtesy of IAIA Museum of Contemporary Native Arts, Santa Fe, NM: H-216. Photo by Jason S. Ordaz.

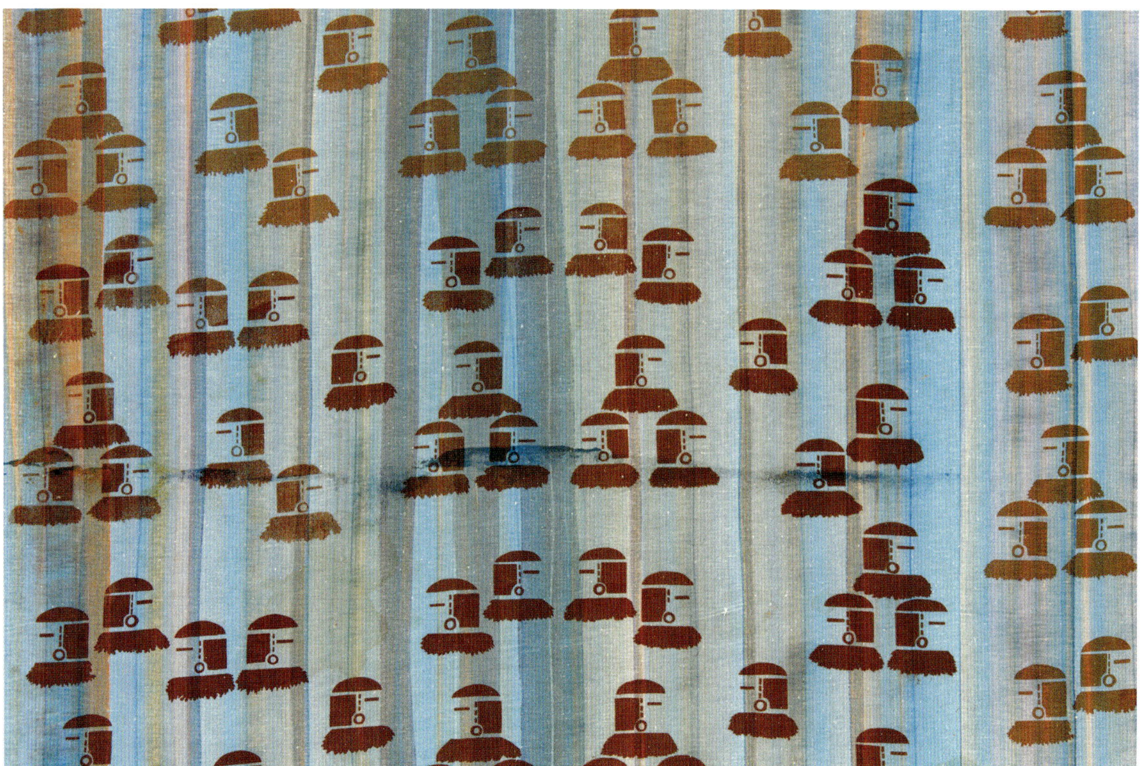

Detail.

Finding a Contemporary Voice: The Legacy of Lloyd Kiva New and IAIA

By Carmen Vendelin, Curator of Art
New Mexico Museum of Art

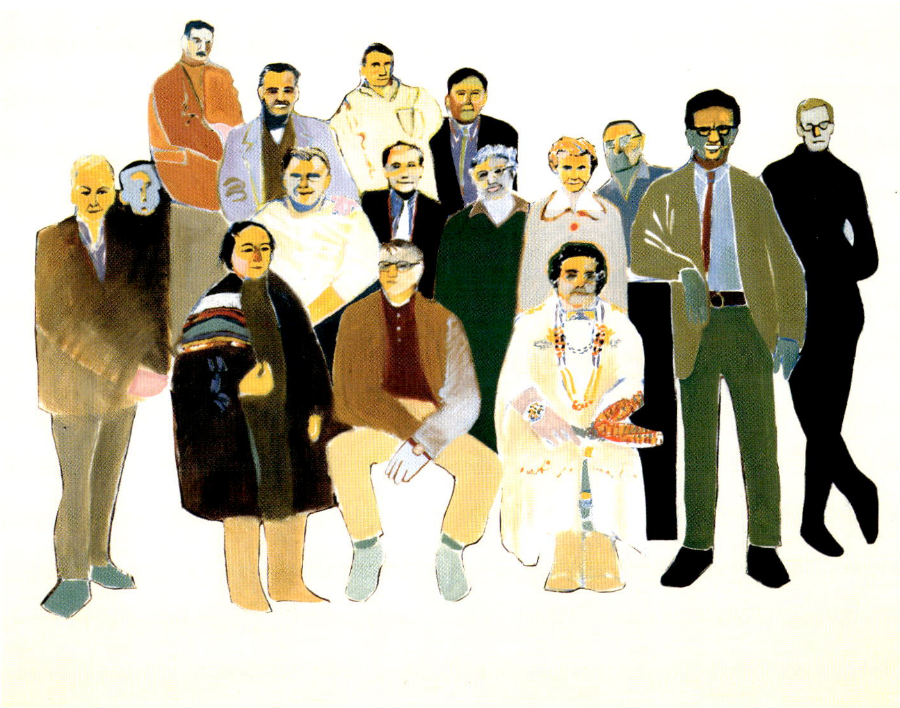

Fritz Scholder, *Arts Faculty at the Institute of American Indian Arts at 4:15pm*, 1968, oil on canvas, 54.5 x 71.5 in. Collection of the New Mexico Museum of Art. Gift of Fritz Scholder, 1968 (2271.23P) © Fritz Scholder Estate. Photo by Blair Clark.

From the school's beginnings in 1962, the Institute of American Indian Arts (IAIA) artists have incorporated cultural and historical narratives, critiques, and forms to communicate indigenous knowledge and creative expression to a wider

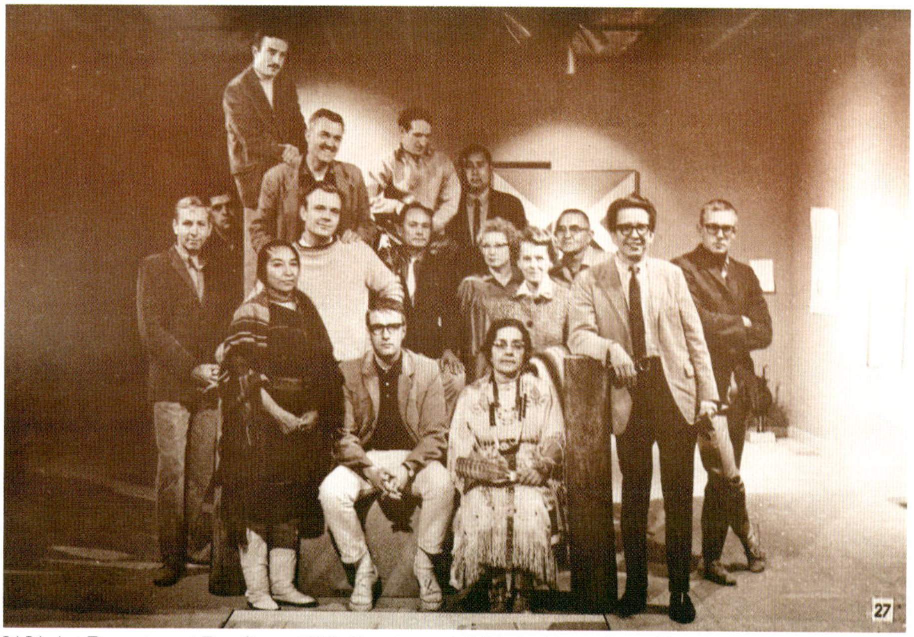

IAIA Art Department Faculty, c. 1966. Courtesy of IAIA Archives, Santa Fe, NM.

art world. The first generation of faculty and students drew inspiration from contemporary art movements of the 1960s, such as Pop and Abstract Expressionism; later generations have participated in Post-Modernism and more recent trends. A group portrait by artist Fritz Scholder in the exhibition *Finding a Contemporary Voice* depicts early faculty members who helped shape the curriculum, mission, and direction of the newly established institute. Among them is Lloyd Kiva New.

Having achieved great professional and artistic success in Arizona, Lloyd Kiva New devoted himself to the role of arts director, and later director, at the newly founded IAIA in Santa Fe, New Mexico, with the goal of empowering individual students to reach their full potential as artists and as people. He believed this could be achieved through a connection to traditional tribal art and culture that would be utilized to create a personal artistic expression.

New did not want his students to feel stifled by pressures to create a certain type of officially sanctioned Indian art. He encouraged students to look at non-indigenous art techniques and forms as a path to creating contemporary Native art. He envisioned IAIA artists engaging in a dialog between cultures—their indigenous heritages and the non-indigenous contemporary mainstream. He asserted that Native artists had a contribution to make to the field of contemporary art. In 1968, New wrote, "Given the opportunity to draw on his own tradition, the Indian artist evolves art forms which are new to the cultural scene, thereby contributing uniquely to the society general."[1] In *Finding a Contemporary Voice,* artwork by former and present IAIA faculty and alumni demonstrates the contribution these artists have made to the larger field of contemporary art.

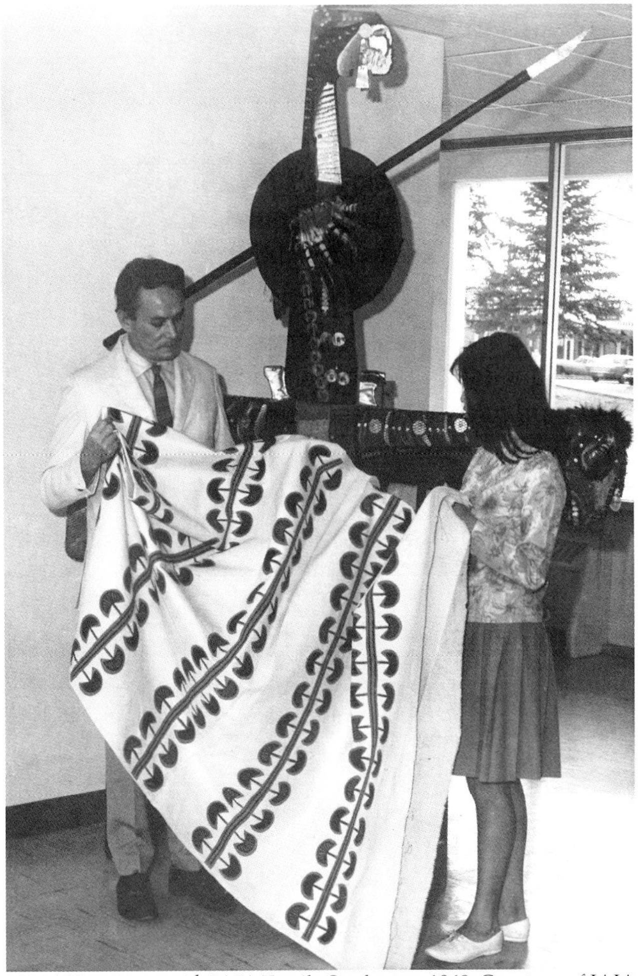

Lloyd Kiva New with IAIA Textile Student, c. 1968. Courtesy of IAIA Archives, Santa Fe, NM.

Santa Fe has long been a tourist center. From the 1880s on, trains and, later, automobiles encouraged an influx of visitors. Local Pueblo

1 New, Lloyd H. "Using Cultural Difference as a Basis for Creative Expression," 1968. Lloyd H. New Papers, IAIA Archives.

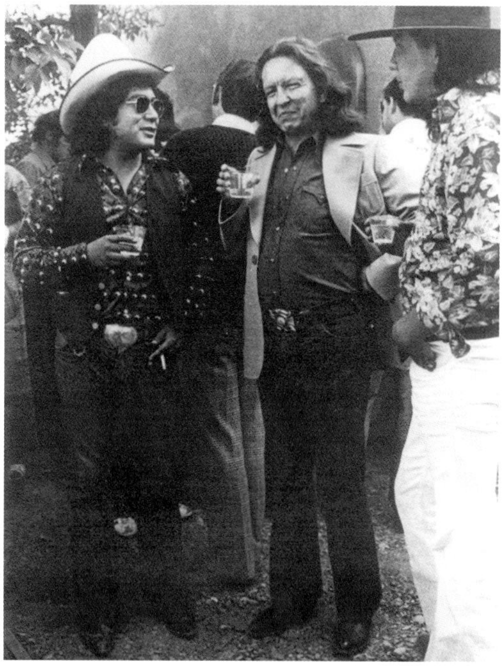

From left; T. C. Cannon (Kiowa/Caddo), Fritz Scholder (Luiseno), and Earl Biss, (Crow) 1976. Courtesy of IAIA Archives, Santa Fe, NM.

and Plains Indian artists developed a variety of pottery, textiles, jewelry, and other objects to meet the market demand and the tastes of non-Native buyers. In the 1930s, Dorothy Dunn taught students at the Santa Fe Indian School to incorporate tribal imagery into a new style of painting.[2] The flattened style was intended to eschew European influences while presenting an "authentic" Indian art, even though the paintings were not part of a tribal tradition. Both of these precedents established a market for Native American art intended for non-indigenous buyers attracted by the forms and motifs of traditional tribal design and culture. Lloyd Kiva New wrote that "the Indian painters of that period [Santa Fe Studio style and self-taught in the years directly preceding the founding of IAIA] were reinforced by white friends and teachers to work in a style which would find acceptance in the white market-place."[3] The insistence that students adhere to particular styles was an idea that New and the newly formed IAIA rejected along with the pressure to cater to a non-indigenous art market.

"Trans-customary" art crosses boundaries between traditional and non-traditional art forms. Art forms based on traditional models created for non-indigenous buyers and the paintings by Santa Fe Indian School artists are, to a degree, trans-customary in that they are not objects used traditionally by the respective tribes. However, the

2 The Studio School at the Santa Fe Indian School closed in 1962, just prior to the opening of IAIA at the same physical facility.

3 *The Institute of American Indian Arts Alumni Exhibition,* (Fort Worth, TX: Amon Carter Museum of Western Art, 1973), 1.

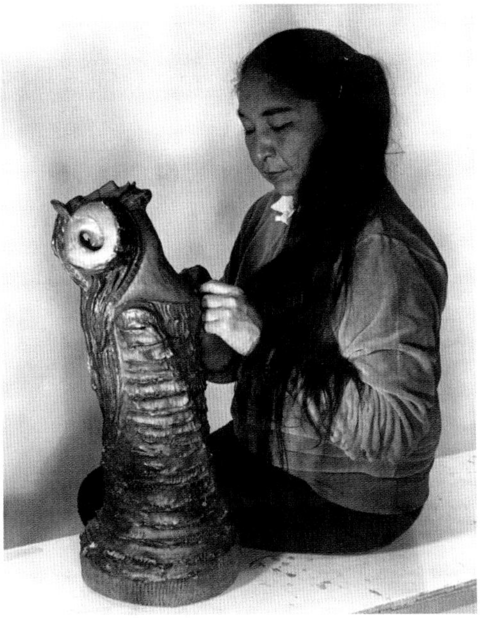

IAIA faculty member Otellie Loloma, (Hopi) c. 1963. Courtesy of IAIA Archives, Santa Fe, NM. Photo by Kay V. Wiest.

engagement with contemporary art practices and styles encouraged at IAIA was far more radical. While there was an established market for traditional Native American art, indigenous artists who engaged with contemporary art movements were taking a leap of faith to pursue art without the same established market of tourist-art buyers and more serious collectors.

IAIA was established by the Bureau of Indian Affairs in 1962. In a 1973 IAIA publication the context is summarized thusly, "The thinking that gave birth to

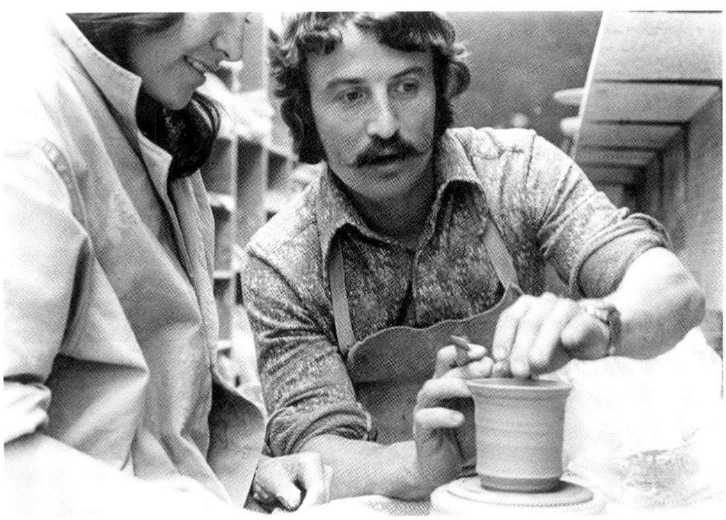

IAIA faculty member Ralph Pardington, c. 1968. Courtesy of IAIA Archives, Santa Fe, NM. Photo by Kay V. Wiest.

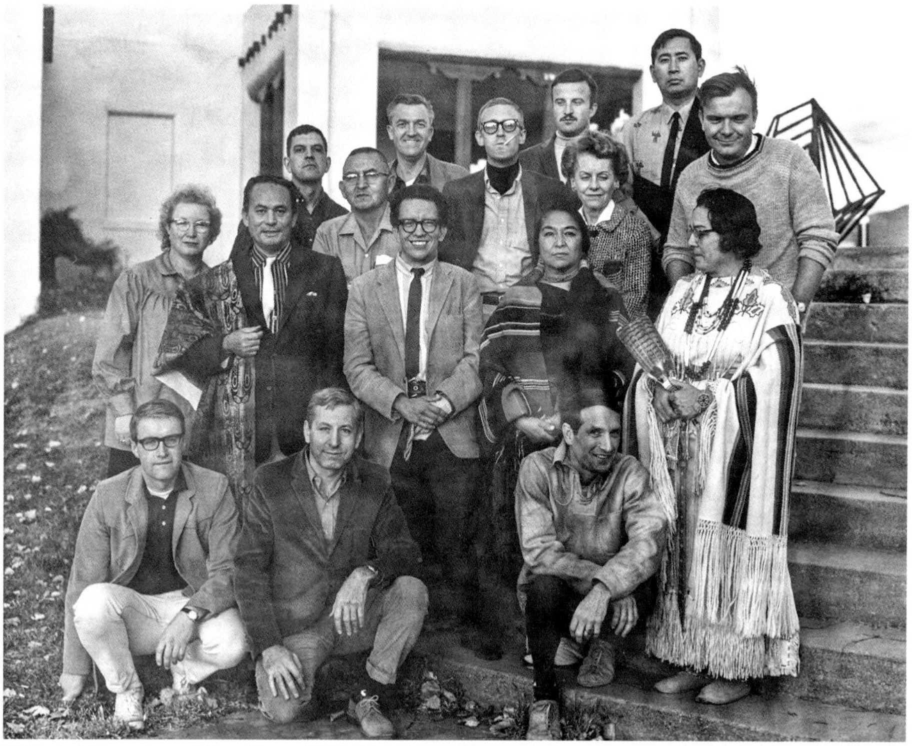

IAIA Art Department Faculty, c. 1966. Courtesy of IAIA Archives, Santa Fe, NM. Photo by Kay V. Wiest.

IAIA was a combination of evolving social attitudes towards Indians, changing federal policies and a social renewal among Indians who had suffered a generation of relocation and assimilation."[4] Native American self-determination was a major issue for many indigenous artists propelled by renewed political activism in the early 1960s. The early years of IAIA occurred during a period of United States history marked with consciousness-raising and civil rights movements. The founding of IAIA also intersected with a significant moment in the history of Western art. Ethnicity and culture, political ideology, feminism, and the inclusion of personal narratives became legitimate forms of expression in mainstream contemporary art. Artists such as Fritz Scholder and his student, T. C. Cannon, addressed Indian stereotypes in art that fit

4 Richard Hill, essays by Nancy Marie Mitchell and Lloyd New, *Creativity is Our Tradition: Three Decades of Contemporary Indian Art at the Institute of American Indian Arts,* (Santa Fe, NM: IAIA Press, 1992), 70.

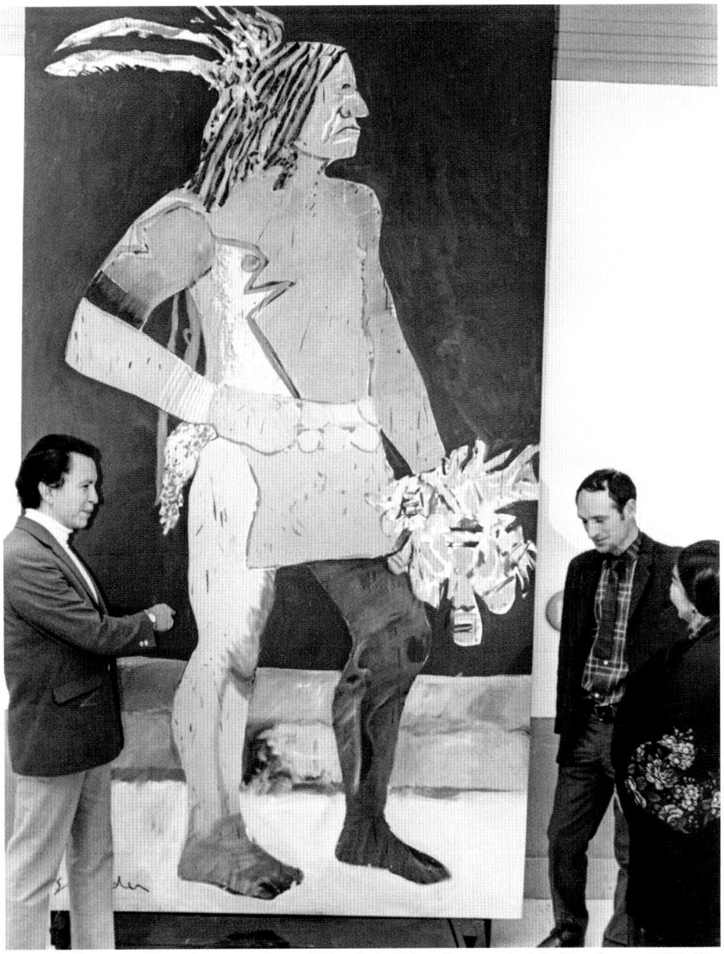

From left: IAIA Faculty members Fritz Scholder, James A. McGrath, and Otellie Loloma, c. 1968. Courtesy of IAIA Archives, Santa Fe, NM. They are standing in front of Fritz Scholder's *Super Indian* c. 1967, oil on canvas. Collection of the New Mexico Museum of Art. Gift of Fritz Scholder, 1969 (2424.23P} © Fritz Scholder Estate.

with then-current Pop Art. Others, such as Neil Parsons, explored more abstract styles that retained referents to tribal culture and identity.

Lloyd Kiva New was appointed Director of IAIA in 1967 and served in that capacity until retiring in 1978. That era saw the Robert Kennedy Senate hearings on Indian education, the formation of the

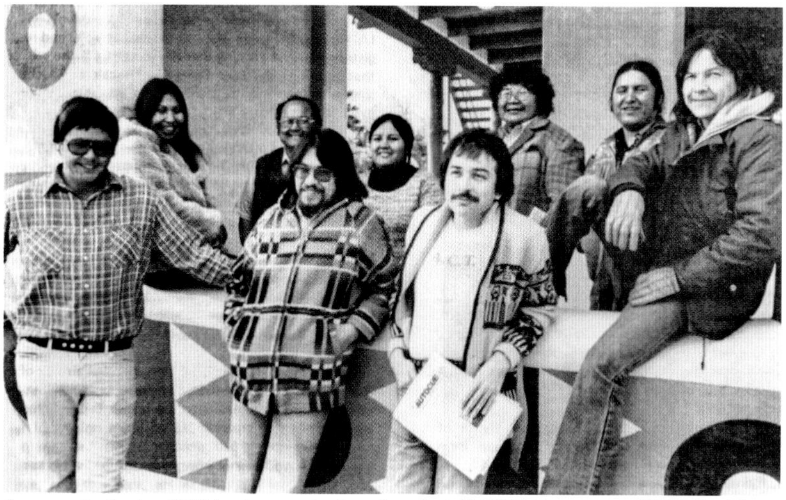

Former students of IAIA return as instructional staff, 1977. Courtesy of IAIA Archives, Santa Fe, NM.

American Indian Movement (AIM), the occupation of Alcatraz, the confrontation at Wounded Knee, and the authorization of the Indian Self-Determination and Education Assistance Act. Artists teaching and studying at IAIA faced opposing forces in a wider contemporary debate regarding the degree to which indigenous artists and their artistic creations should assimilate or resist assimilation into mainstream American society.

Now over fifty-years old, scholars have enough historical perspective to examine the early days of IAIA in greater context. Younger artists continue to use art as a vehicle for interrogating issues of Native American identity through traditional and contemporary styles and techniques. For example, former faculty member Melanie Yazzie presents post-colonial women's issues and alumna Hulleah Tsinhnahjinnie utilizes historical and family photographs to explore the complexities of identity in being both a member of the Navajo Nation and a United States citizen. IAIA artists have found a voice through modes of Pop Art and abstraction; by re-appropriating and critiquing historical narratives; and concerns for matters such as environmental politics and land rights. Looking at the issues of identity still being raised in contemporary Native American art, it is clear that the artwork of the 1960s and 1970s began a conversation that continues to this day. The artworks included in the exhibition demonstrate what individual artists brought to IAIA and what they took away from their experience there. In their work, the legacy of Lloyd Kiva New's vision lives on.

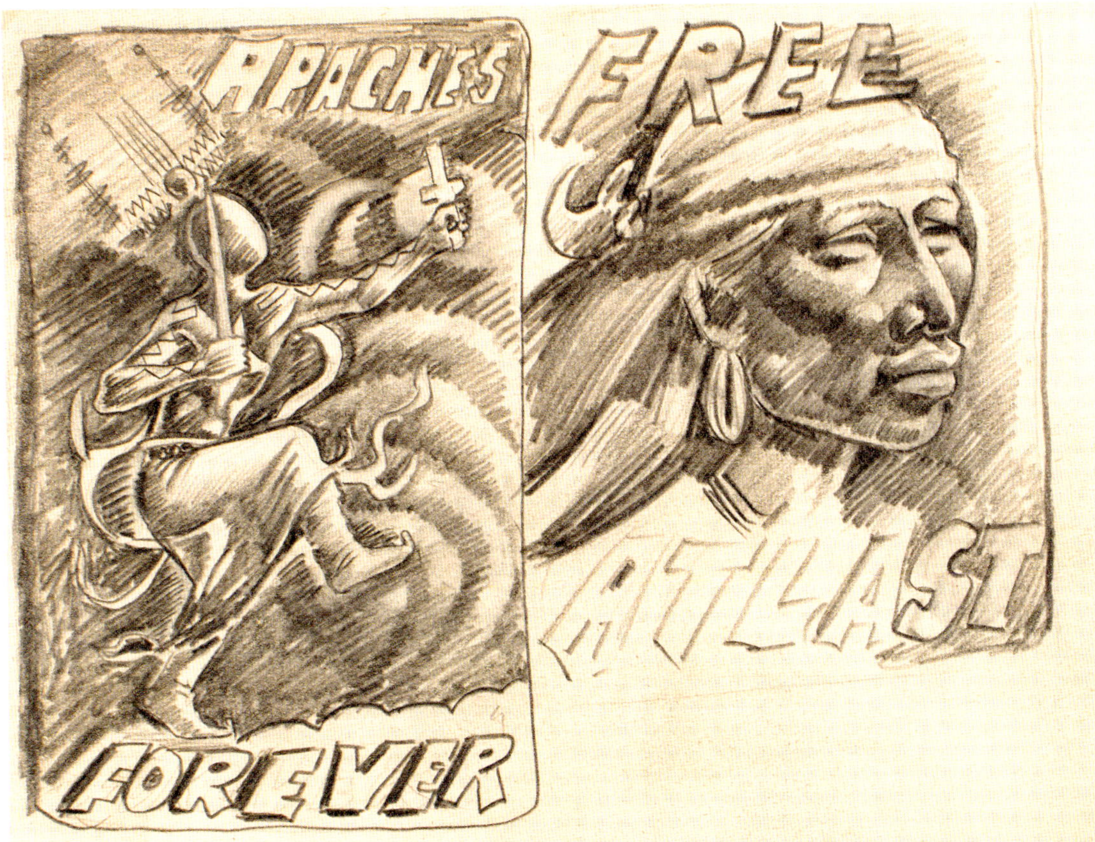

Allan Houser, *Apache Forever / Free at Last* c. 1964, pencil on paper, 8.9375 x 11.9375 in. Collection of the Allan Houser Foundation © Chiinde LLC.

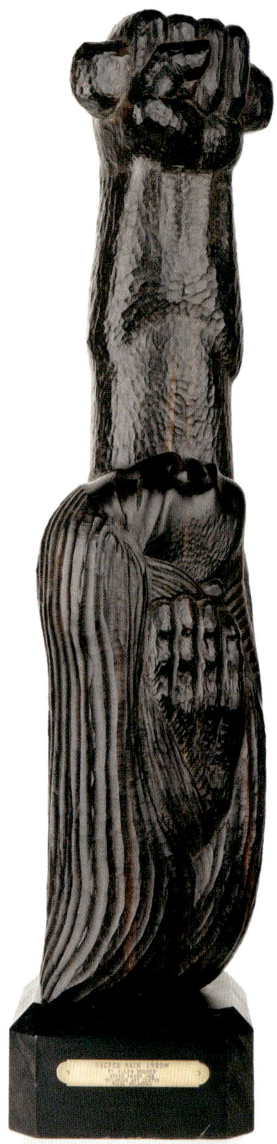

Allan Houser, *Sacred Rain Arrow (ebony)*, 1968, wood (ebony), 28 x 6 x 6 in. Collection of the Allan Houser Foundation © Chiinde LLC.

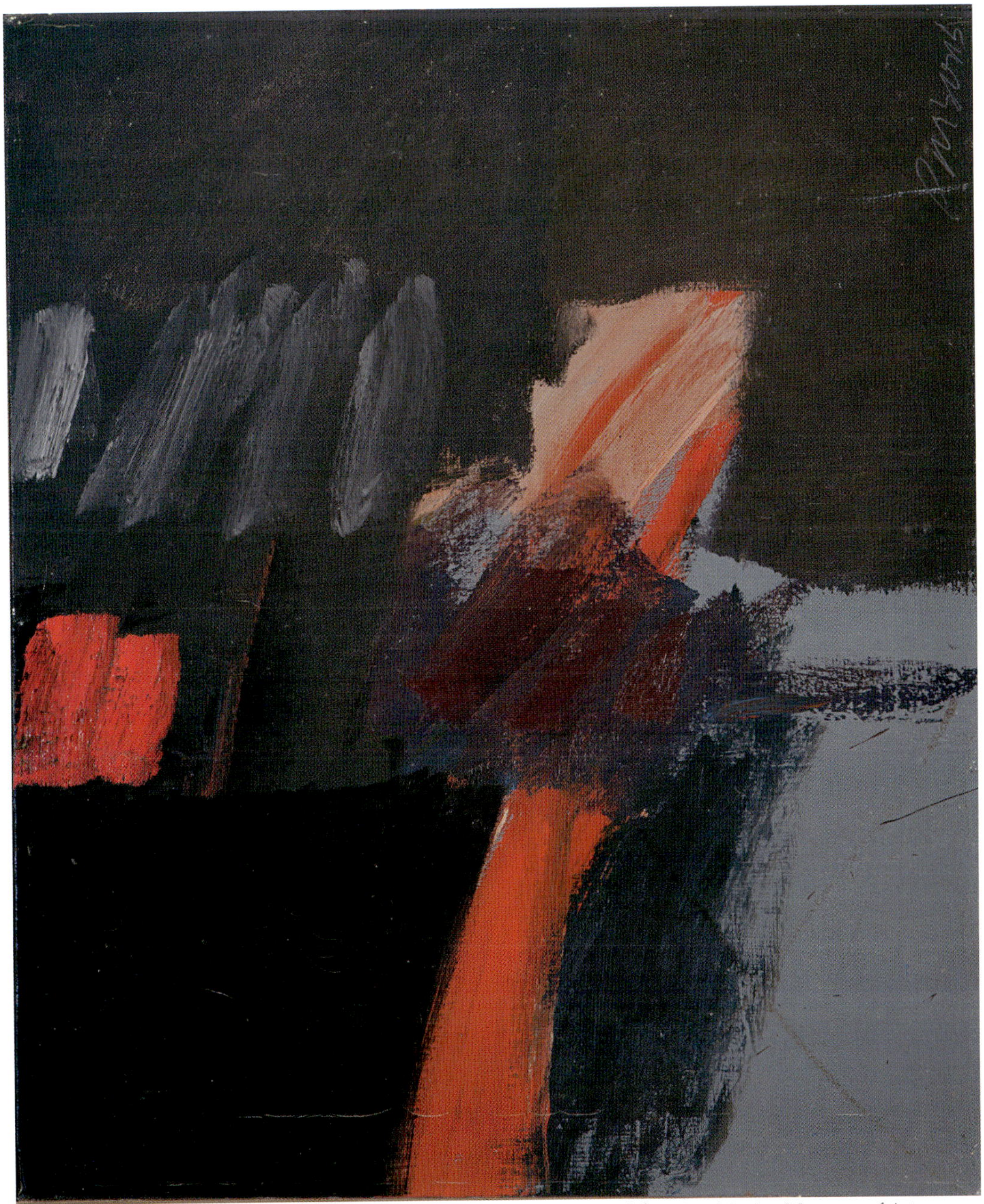

Neil Parsons, *Retablo Image,* n.d. oil on canvas, 24 x 20 in. Collection of the New Mexico Museum of Art. Gift of Neil Parsons, 1969 (2407.23P) © Neil Parsons. Photo by Blair Clark.

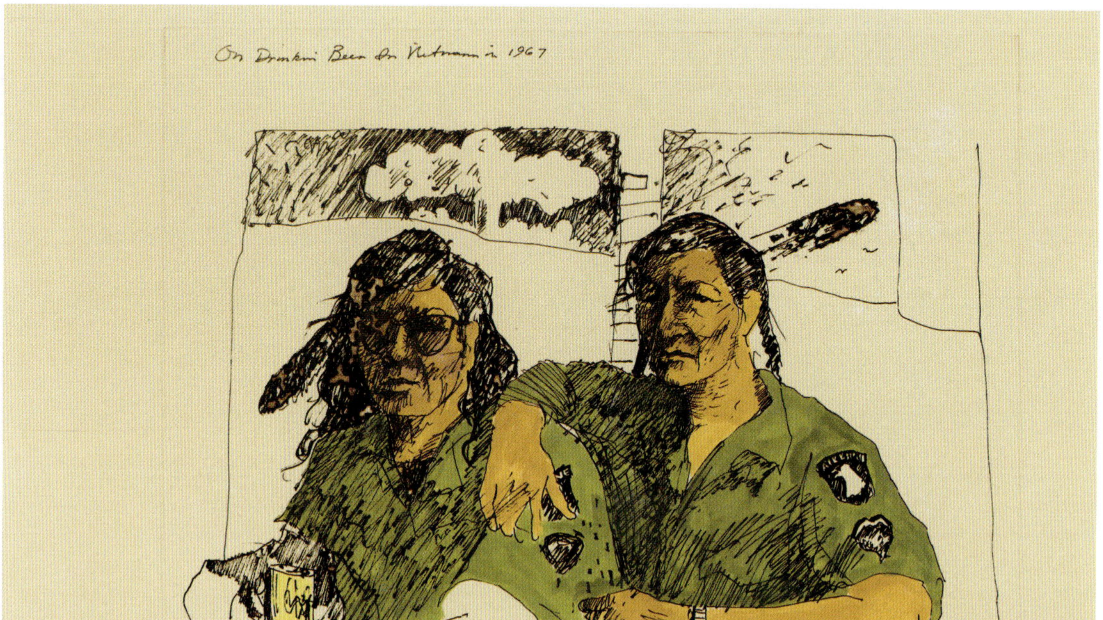

T. C. Cannon, *On Drinking Beer in Vietnam in 1967,* ed. 6/100, 1971, lithograph, Gift of Kenneth French, Courtesy of IAIA Museum of Contemporary Native Arts, Santa Fe, NM (CD-33). Photo by Jason Ordaz.

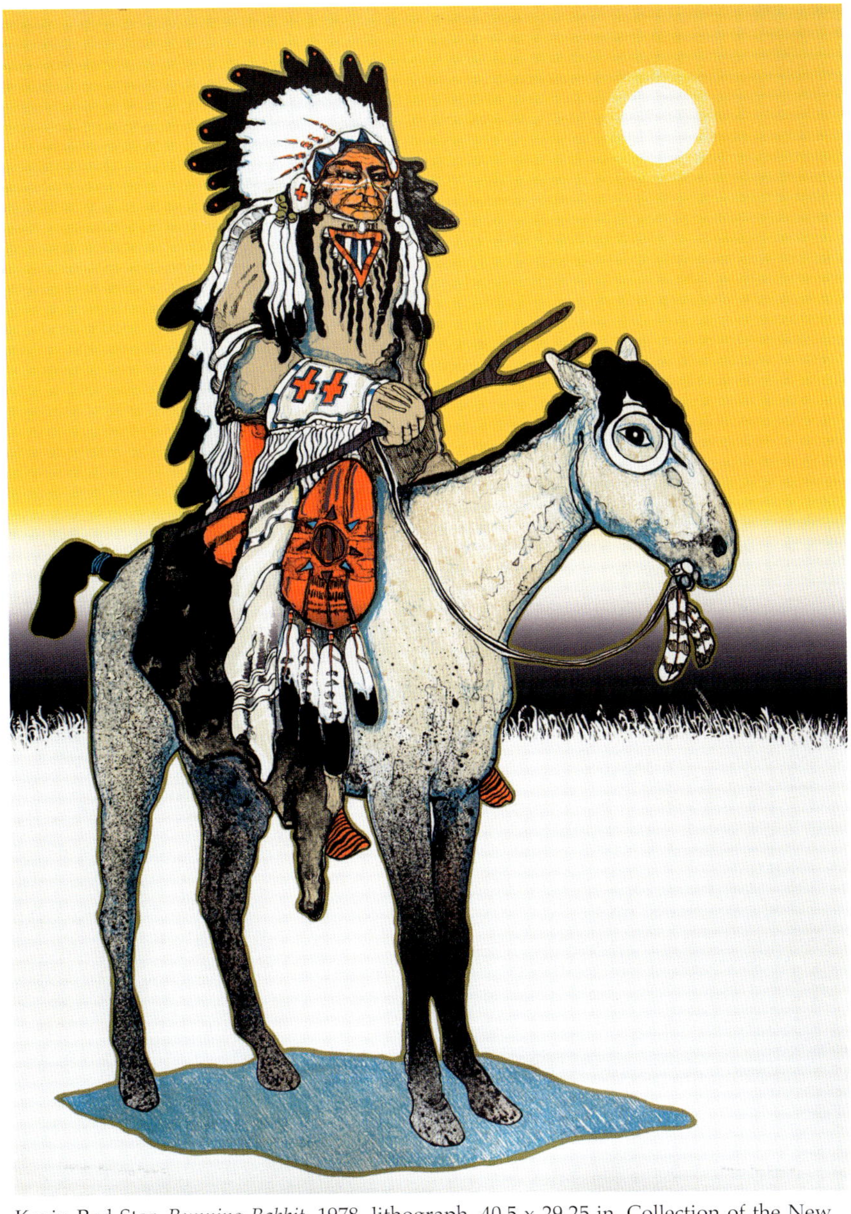

Kevin Red Star, *Running Rabbit*, 1978, lithograph, 40.5 x 29.25 in. Collection of the New Mexico Museum of Art. Gift of Elizabeth and Duncan Boeckman, 2000 (2000.7.2) © Kevin Red Star. Photo by Blair Clark.

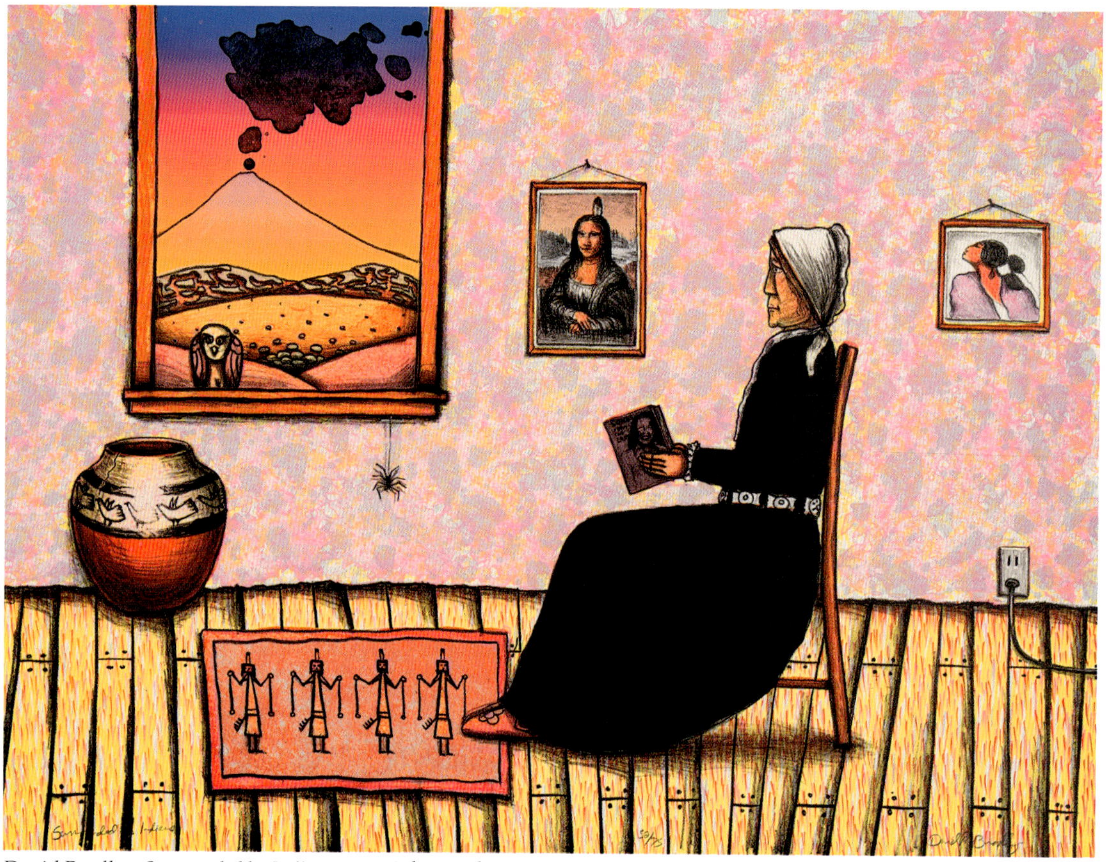

David Bradley, *Surrounded by Indians*, 1982, lithograph, 22.25 × 30 in. Collection of the New Mexico Museum of Art. Gift of Mr. and Mrs. David C. Smith, 1985 (1985.208.1) © David Bradley. Photo by Blair Clark.

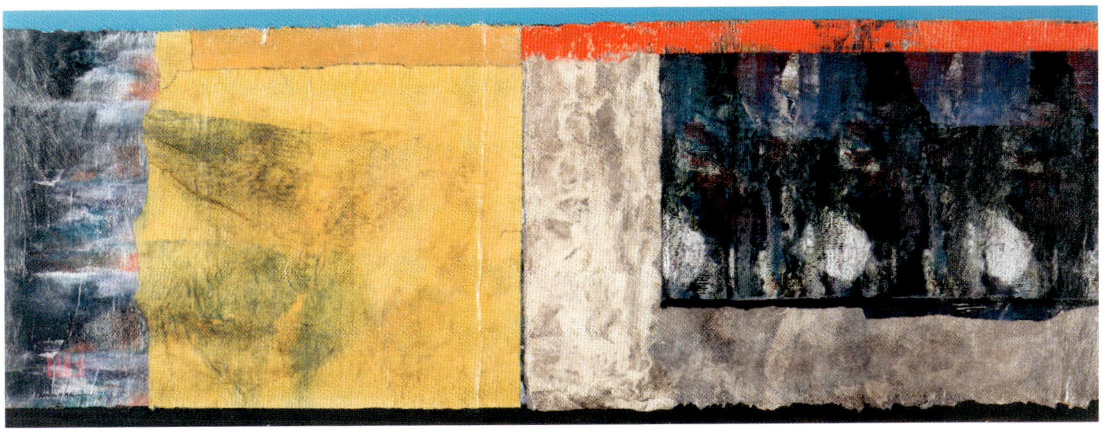

Dan Namingha, *Reservation: Landscape Series,* 1989, mixed media collage, 13.5 x 40 in. Collection of the New Mexico Museum of Art. Gift from Niman Fine Art, 1991 (1991.98.1) © Dan Namingha. Photo by Blair Clark.

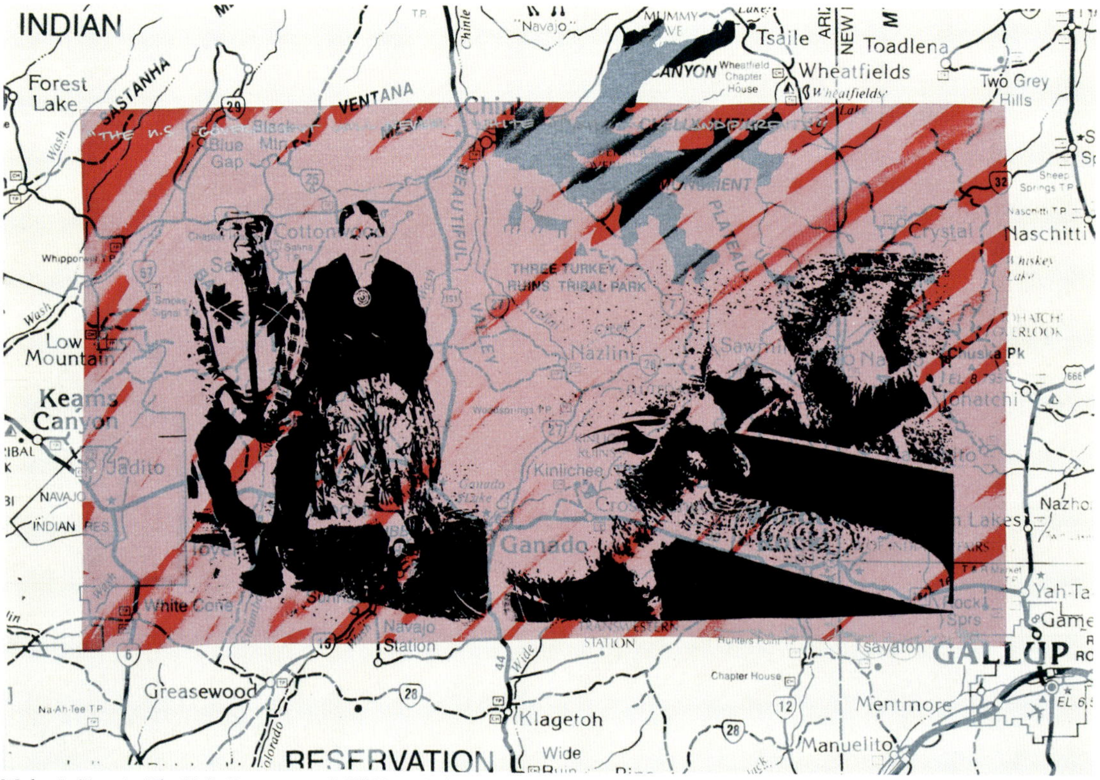

Melanie Yazzie, *The U.S. Government Will Never White Wash My Grandparents,* 1992, screen print, 14.9375 x 21.875 in. Collection of the New Mexico Museum of Art. Gift of Lucy R. Lippard, 1999 (1999.15.213) © Melanie Yazzie. Photo by Blair Clark.

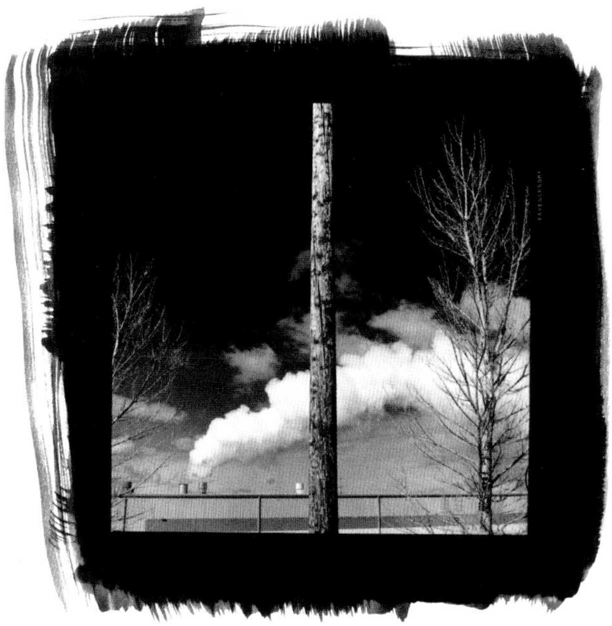

Page One

Over the years I've been cordially invited to participate in a number of exhibitions, many with titles such as Spirit Capture, Praising the Spirit, Spirit of Native America, and so on.

I must be a spiritual expert, so I set out on a quest to gather spiritual power.

On my sacred journey, I found this sacred power pole. The curators will be happy.

Larry McNeil, *Sacred Power Pole,* from *The Sacred Series,* 1997 (printed 2016) Digital print after palladium original 22 x 35 in. © Larry McNeil, All Rights Reserved, 1998

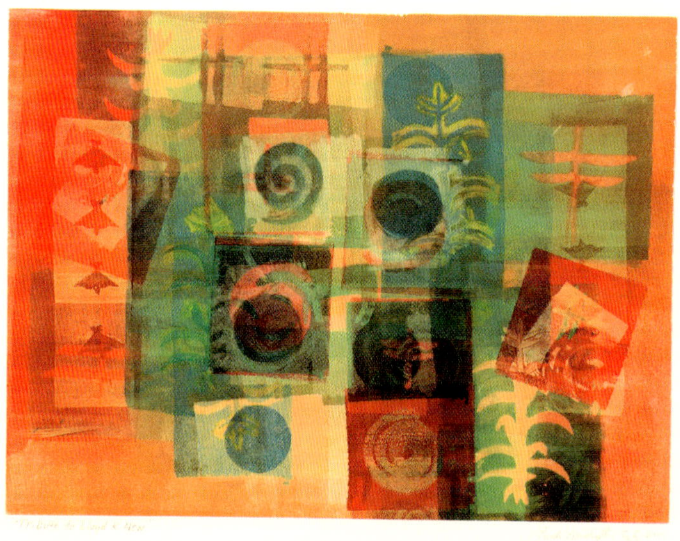

Linda Lomahaftewa, *Tribute to Lloyd K. New*, 2001, monotype on paper, 22 x 26 in., Courtesy of IAIA Museum of Contemporary Native Arts, Santa Fe, NM (H-401). Photo by Jason S. Ordaz.

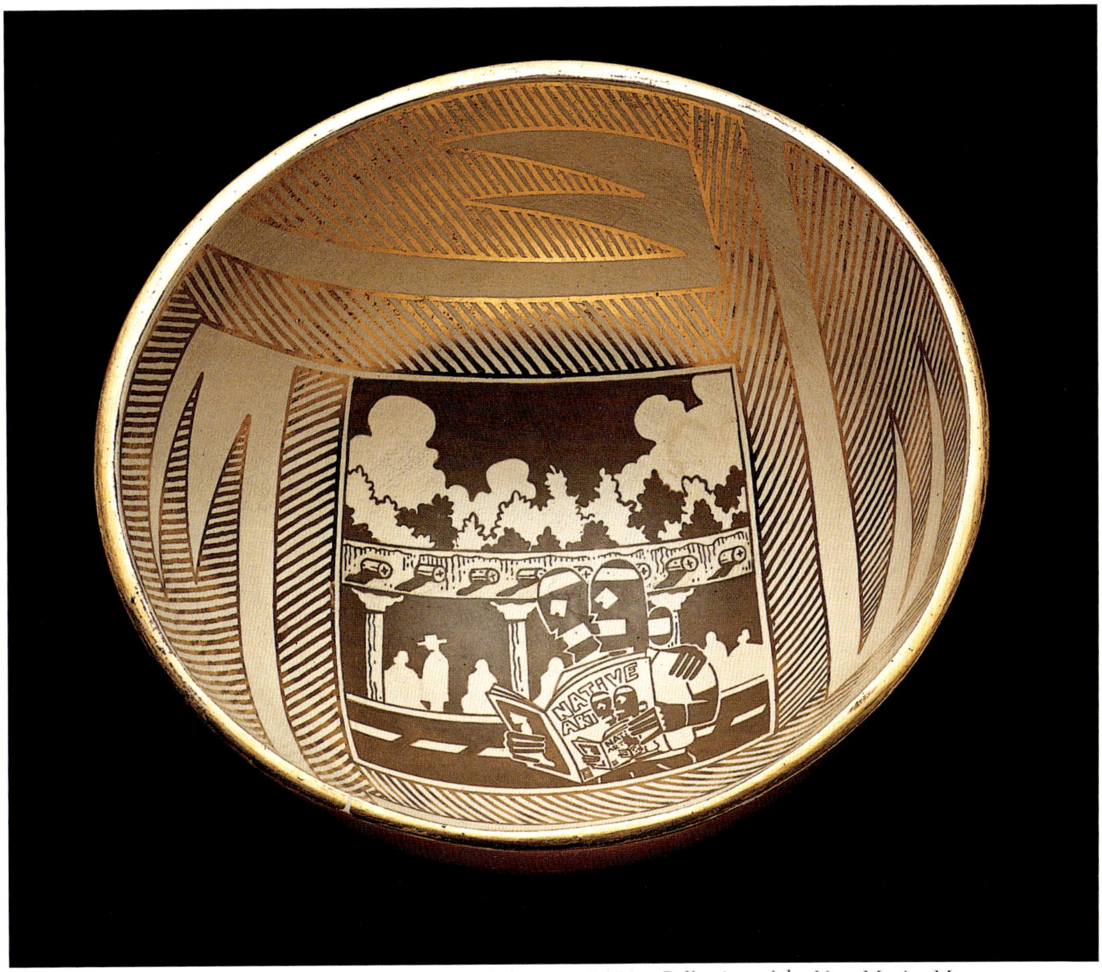

Diego Romero, *Double Take,* 2002, gold gilt, paint and clay, 11 x 5.25 in. Collection of the New Mexico Museum of Art. Museum purchase with funds from the Herzstein Family Acquisition Endowment Fund, 2003 (2003.14.1) © Diego Romero. Photo by Blair Clark.

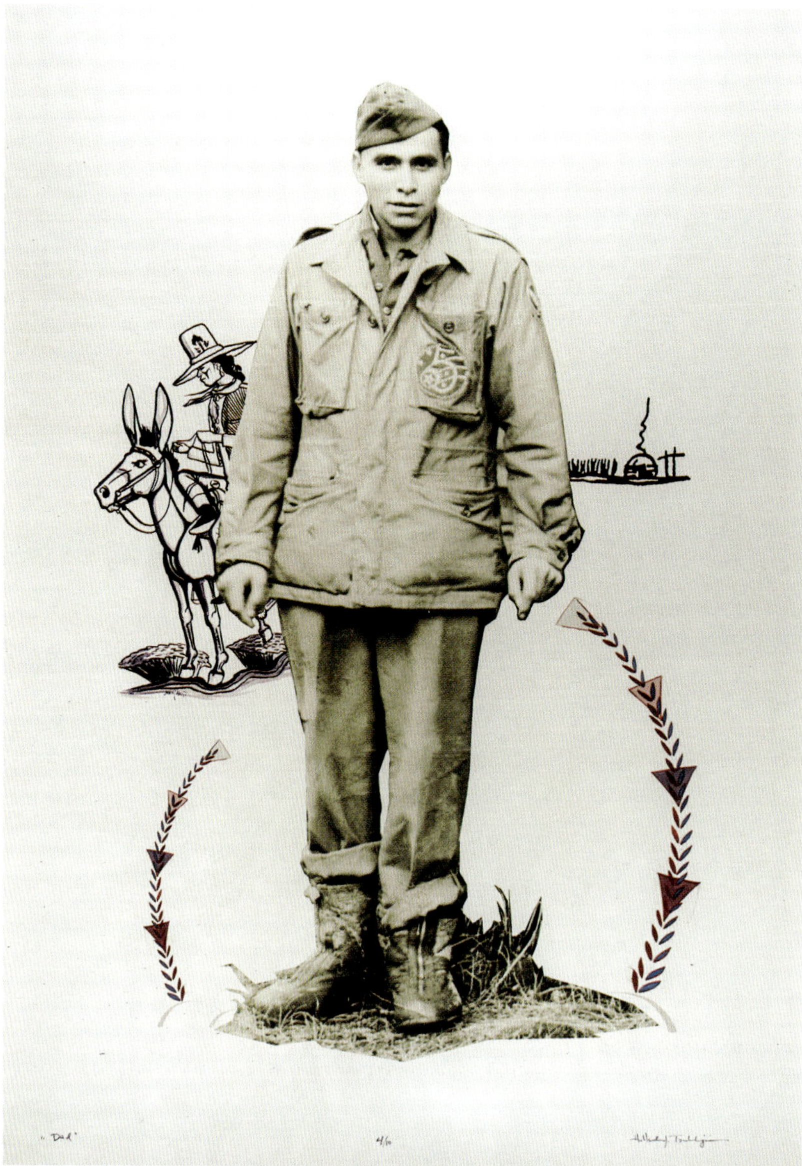

Hulleah J. Tsinhnahjinnie, *Dad*, 2003 (printed 2013), platinum lambda print, 33.9375 × 23.9375 in. Collection of the New Mexico Museum of Art. Museum purchase with funds from the Clinton King Purchase Award, 2014 (2014.3.1) © Hulleah J. Tsinhnahjinnie. Photo by Blair Clark.

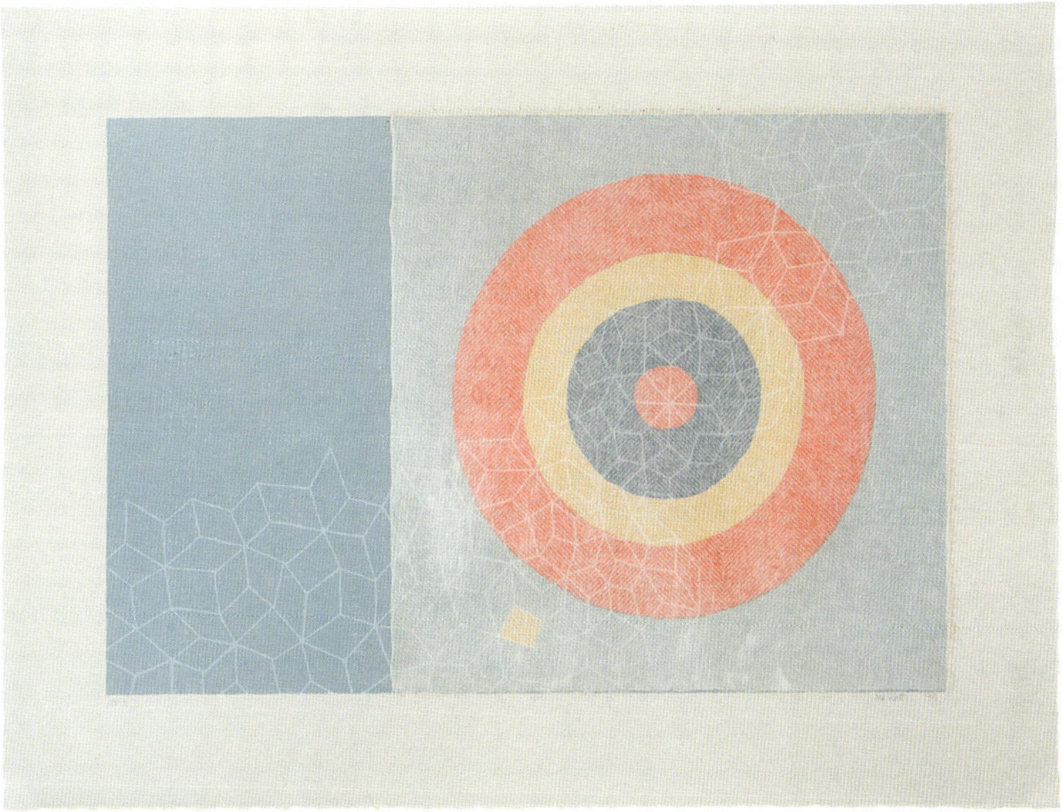

Marie Watt, *Transit*, 2004, lithograph, 15.875 x 23.875 in. Collection of the New Mexico Museum of Art. Museum purchase with funds from Phyllis Sloane, 2007 (2007.20) © Marie Watt. Photo by Blair Clark.

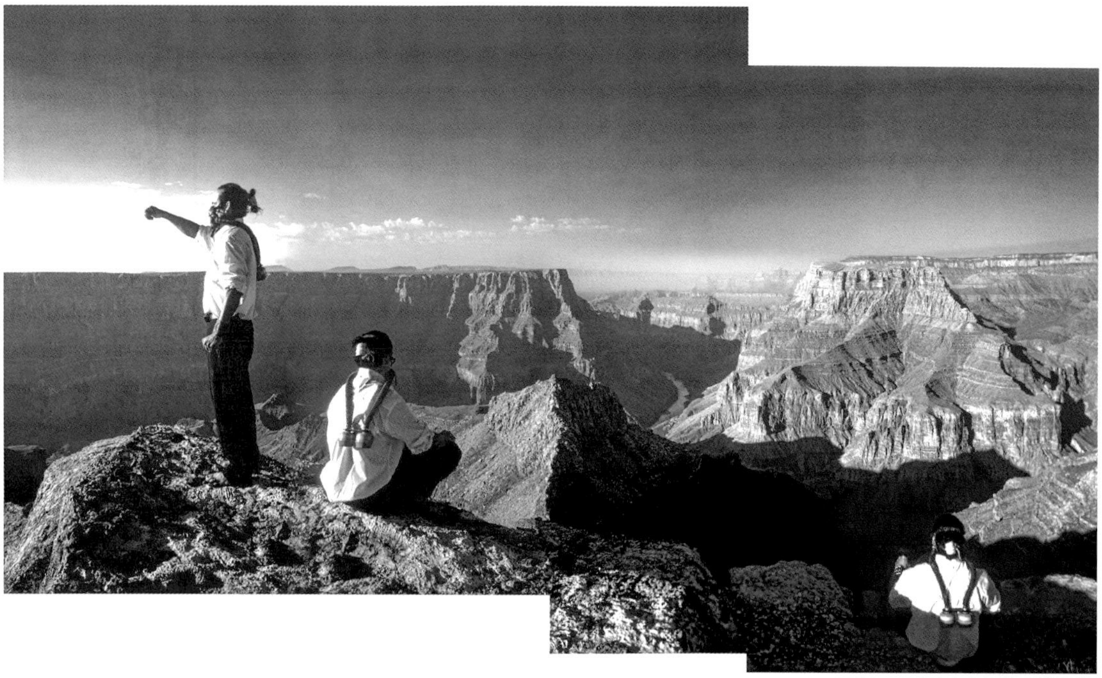

Will Wilson, *Auto Immune Response #2*, 2005, pigment print, 23.5 x 40.375 in. Collection of the New Mexico Museum of Art. Museum purchase with funds from the Clinton King Purchase Award, 2013 (2013.22) © Will Wilson.

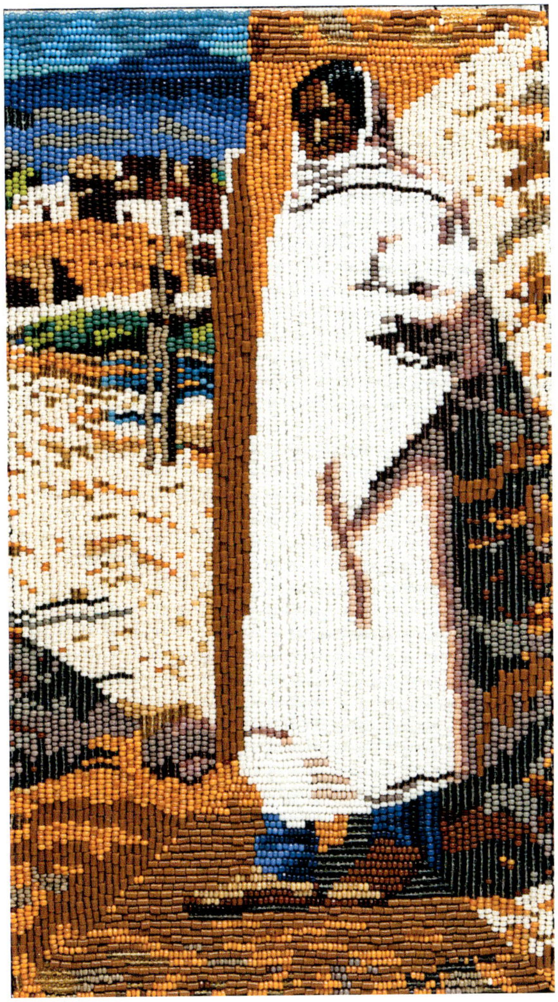

Marcus Amerman, *Back to the Blanket*, 2008, size 13 cut beads on fabric, 8.125 x 4.625 in. Collection of the New Mexico Museum of Art. Museum purchase with funds from Charmay B. Allred, Jeff and Darlene Anderson, the Clinton King Purchase Award and Jane and Bill Buchsbaum, 2008 (2008.50) © Marcus Amerman. Photo by Blair Clark.

Afterword

By Nancy Marie Mithlo, Ph.D. (Chiricahua Apache)

I remember the first time I spoke with Lloyd New over thirty years ago. I called from a heavy beige landline phone that sat under an old-fashioned reading lamp. On the desk was hand-made sign warning students of a strict five minute call limit. It is certain that I spoke too fast. I had a habit of doing that when I was nervous. A museum studies student at the Institute of American Indian Arts, I was curious about New's archives and wanted to know more. On the phone, Lloyd had agreed to let me do an interview with him in another week and I was completely elated. I could not believe I had actually spoken with the man whose work I so admired. After placing the phone down, I remember looking out across the bare winter campus from those tall upstairs windows at the old IAIA Library, feeling that my life had somehow changed. I think Lloyd had that impact on a lot of people.

Now as a teacher and researcher, I often ask myself, "What would Lloyd do?" How would Mr. New interpret the latest Facebook news on cultural appropriations? Would he be angry that Bethany Yellowtail's designs from her Crow Pop Collection were ripped off? What quote would he provide for Indian Country Today's online news feed? What would Lloyd say about Project Runway or Beyoncé's Lemonade? Would he attend the Native American and Indigenous Studies meetings in

Hawaii this spring? Perhaps he would be too busy with his new 3-D printed jewelry line or his designer scarves. If Lloyd were a twenty year old again, at what museum would he have his "ah-ha" moment, if not the Art Institute of Chicago? Would it be Los Angeles County Museum of Art or perhaps the Tate Modern? Would he be shocked to learn that in 2016 American Indian professors represent less than 1% of faculty nationally? Would he author a paper on the 67% graduation rate of American Indian/Alaskan Native high school students, the lowest of any racial/ethnic group in the country?[1] Might he launch a new policy institute?

I wonder about all of this because as important as Lloyd's artistic influence was and continues to be, I believe it is his intellectual contribution that will serve to inform the next seven generations. How do we best describe this aspect of the man? Is it simply as he writes in "Using Cultural Difference as a Basis for Creative Expression" (1968) that "cultural differences are good"? And is this belief in the worth of cultural knowledge a methodology, an attitude, or a philosophy? How does New's legacy fit into his own cultural environment? What were the social and political realities of his lifetime?

In 1916 when Lloyd was born, the U.S. government had just passed yet another restrictive legal mandate supporting the national guardianship of Native nations in "The United States vs. Nice." Also in 1916, George Gustav Heye opened the Museum of the American Indian in New York City. Clearly, the schizophrenic U.S. policy of simultaneously destroying and preserving American Indian life and culture was still active in Mr. New's youth. His productive career in the arts spanned the length of two generations – years thought of now as the transformative post-war period of American modernity and achievement. And yet for American Indians, the second half of the last century were years of disenfranchisement and continued struggle for basic human rights such as adequate health care, education, housing, and cultural continuation dependent on access to land, language, and religion. Throughout this historic period, Lloyd would serve as a key architect in building progressive educational models, museum and arts programming, economic development initiatives, and psychological

1 2014 Native Youth Repport. Executive Office of the President, The White House. December 2014. www.whitehouse.cov/sites/default/files/docs/20141129nativeyouthreport_final.pdf.

health and well-being promotion in Native communities. He believed in the power of culture multiplied; his was an expansive vision that included both political and social dimensions.

I will draw from just two examples of how I experienced New's contributions. Lloyd was an early participant in discussions leading to the Venice Biennale art exhibits I have been a part of for the last twenty years. For the first edition in 1999, our group of artists, educators, and activists had considered asking the Phillip Morris corporation for funding to support the show. Members were concerned however about the corporation's reputation, its obvious health-related impacts on consumers of tobacco, and its questionable business practices. Lloyd held sway from his white couch in the front living room of his home where we so often met, "I'll be damned if we let them take tobacco from the Indians!" He wanted us to go forward with the grant request of course, because the original plant was ours to begin with and no one had ever taken our sacred medicine away. He advocated sovereignty before we even had the words to describe this approach.[2]

Lloyd's interpretation of culture was also affective in nature. He advanced his own brand of psychological well-being based on self-acceptance and love. Lloyd allowed us to consider the possibility of a life that was comfortable, fulfilling even, and without guilt. "I'm not going to apologize for living in a nice home or driving a nice car," he confidently advised me. Many of my generation, the baby boomers living with the trauma of our parent's boarding school experiences, still struggle with a type of "survivor syndrome." We were not imprisoned, we were not beaten, so what right do we have to a secure, contented life? In an era often defined as a period of self-doubt for Indian people, Lloyd offered the cool option. Like a classic black and white 1950s movie, in which everyone dresses splendidly, says, "swell," and refers to each other as "kids," Lloyd's world was upbeat and positive. The darkness of poverty, abuse, and despair was not apparent in Lloyd's approach to education and the arts. He was clearly aware of the often-harsh realities of Native communities, but he presented a different reality, one that was colorful, self-assured and importantly, educated.

2 Our collective was not successful in obtaining grant support from Phillip Morris, now the Altria Group.

Lloyd New's contributions to education continue to provoke and inspire. At the heart of the "cultural difference" philosophy is the question of training – Western and Indigenous. When New stepped into the role of co-directing the Southwest Indian Arts and Crafts Workshop in 1959, he faced long-standing core contradictions built on racial biases. Would Indian art be best served by an approach that encouraged deep engagement in historic forms or would Indian art students benefit from non-Native instruction, including immersion in non-Native art forms, materials, and instructors? The original Rockefeller proposal appears fairly straightforward in their agenda, which can only be interpreted as assimilationist in stating, "[I]f Southwestern Indian art is to survive, it must take new directions. Few believe that the force needed to produce this impetus could be generated wholly within Indian cultural circles. Clearly the future of Indian art hinges not on the talents and efforts of established Indian artists and craftsmen but on the direction in which the budding talent of younger Indians is guided." The report calls for the "relationship between young Indian artists and non-Indian professional groups capable of assisting the development of indigenous talent."[3]

This argument that Native art students must be immersed in the non-Indian world to succeed is of course flawed in several respects: A) the notion of Native arts as somehow disappearing (the field's "survival" at stake); B) the idea that established Indian artists are incapable of innovation, and; C) the proposal that only non-Native professionals can effectively educate Indian artists (the white savior narrative). This Western-centric approach clearly diminishes the power and worth of Indigenous knowledge.

New was cited in the Rockefeller proposal as a cultural advocate stating, "Let's be more concerned with the evolution of artists than of art products. Let's see that the young Indian realizes the value of his great and wonderful traditions as the springboard for his own personal creative ideas. Indian art of the future will be in new forms, produced in new media and with new technological methods. The end result will be as Indian as the Indian."[4] It is important to note here Lloyd's

3 The University of Arizona, "A Proposal for an Exploratory Workshop in Art for Talented Younger Indians." Submitted to the Rockefeller Foundation, October 15, 1959.

4 Ibid.

insistence that the art product (a commodity of sorts) should rightly be separated from the producer (contemporaneous American Indian communities). The evolution of the artist as a coeval human being, a person with dignity and worth, was the primary goal, not the value and investment in the product known as "Southwestern Indian art."

Problematically, New's words ("new forms," "new media," and "personal creative ideas") were apparently misinterpreted by government officials. His enthusiasm for freeing Indian artists from constricting commercial boundaries was interpreted as a need to discount the primacy of Native artists working in Native contexts. Clearly, the art product and the artisan were conflated in a rigid equation whereby what might be considered Modern art could only be taught by someone considered a modern person, meaning a non-Native instructor.

New struggled with what he called an apparent "lack of unanimity of opinion as to what the proper emphasis should be..." between Western and Native instruction – instruction both in terms of the instructor's ethnicity and the content of the curriculum. Declaring that "INDIAN ART, whatever its variations from ART…is the very core of this project," (capitalization here his own), New concluded, "the emphasis on all instructional procedure should be on laying a firm identification with each student in his own cultural accomplishments first."[5]

By the end of the first full year of the Southwest Indian Arts and Crafts Workshop in 1961, New was adamant, "While our stated purpose is to see how young Indian artists and craftsmen react to formal, instructional methods designed to help them discover individual creative powers, and to learn about art in its universal sense, are we not primarily interested in seeing how much of the resulting expression may be uniquely Indian, reflecting the particular qualities of a different culture? ... It worries me…that we sometimes take the attitude…that our first responsibility is to fit the Indian artist into the world of art in general, and the sooner he gets into the mainstream of the universality of art, the better off he will be…I sense this as the

5 Lloyd Kiva, July 28, 1960. IAIA Archives.

biggest unresolved difference of philosophy amongst the staff."[6]

I cite these documents at length to reflect on the very difficult task, that we are still struggling with, of instructing Native art students under opposing value systems.[7] I do not think these divergent standards have been adequately assessed to date in a meaningful fashion. We lack core resources, including image banks, graduate programs, definitive texts, academic journals, and professional organizations that can accurately articulate the complex realities of contemporary Native arts. We need academic resources that do not alienate Native art students by their use of chronological and regional constraints, that do not speak in the past tense and that recognize that American Indian artists have always been modern. The "biggest unresolved difference of philosophy" seems ever present.

What would Lloyd do?

I think Lloyd would articulate clearly his core belief in the reality of Native peoples as contemporaneous. Collectively, we can now confidently reaffirm that: A) Modernism as an art form (geometrics, non-linear figuration) is innately of Native manufacture; B) Modernism as a societal value (a belief in "science" and "progress") is innately counter to Indigenous values; and C) Native peoples engaged in Modernism as an art form are not inherently agreeing to the social values of Modernism (individualism, competition, capitalism). There, we said it. Again. Let's hope some folks listen well.

Lloyd, you were right of course, "Let's be more concerned with the evolution of artists than of art products." Our seventh generation awaits. Will we be ready?

6 Lloyd Kiva, "Comments on Southwest Indian Arts and Crafts Project, University of Arizona…2nd year, 1961." The culmination of this educational approach was summarized in New's manifesto "Using Cultural Difference as a Basis for Creative Expression," February 5, 1962.

7 For more reading on the conflicts of culturally-informed arts curriculum see Karen Kosadsa's 2002 dissertation "Critical Sights/Sites: Art Pedagogy and Settler Colonialism in Hawai'i." University of Rochester, Program in Visual and Cultural Studies.

Acknowledgements

The Museum of Indian Arts and Culture gratefully acknowledges the following donors for their support of our exhibitions and programming. Special thanks to the friends of Lloyd Kiva New and the Museum of New Mexico Foundation for their dedicated support of this project.

Director's Leadership Fund
Charmay B. Allred
Joy and Howard Berlin
Nancy and Richard Bloch
Benjamin Crane
Dobkin Family Foundation in honor of Leroy Garcia
John P. C. Duncan and Anita M. Sarafa
Karen Freeman
Friends of Indian Art
Hutson-Wiley and Echevarria Foundation, Inc.
Maureen McCarthy and John Schoemer
Ashlyn and Dan Perry
Cindi and Michael Pettit
Governor and Mrs. Bill Richardson
Harriet and Karl Schreiner
Judy and Bob Sherman
William and Salomé Scanlan Family Foundation
Gil Waldman and Christy Vezolles
Eileen A. Wells

Exhibitions Development/Education Funds
Elie Abemayor
Catherine Allen and Paul Rooker
Ann Griffith Ash
JoAnn and Bob Balzer
John Berl and Bob Bauernschmitt

Gail and Joel Bernstein
Dorothy Bracey and Tom Johnson
Lynn G. and Norman Brown
Jane and Bill Buchsbaum
Buffalo Bill Center of the West & Plains Indian Museum Advisory Board
John M. Campbell, Jr.
Susan and Conrad De Jong
Sharon Curran-Wescott and Earle Wescott
Rosalind and Lowell Doherty
Joan C. Donner
Ardith Eicher and David Rashin
Candace and Bert Forbes
Fort Sill Apache Tribe
Andrew Freeman and Peggy Mainor
Helen C. Gabriel
Mary and Thomas James
Anita Katz
Mary Anne and Bruce Larsen
Enid Margolies
Susan and Philip Marineau
Jenny Auger Maw and Gilbert Maw
Linda and Philip McGowan
Beverly and Mike Morris
Navajo Arts and Crafts Enterprise
Judith and Jan Novak
Yara and Gerald Pitchford
Keith and Frauke Roth
Kathleen and Morton Sachs
Roy Schneiderman and Susie Chang
Beth and Richard Schnieders
Joan and Michael Snader
Southwestern Association for Indian Arts
Carol Warren
Merja and Axel Weinreich
Brenda Whorton
Sharon and Don Wright

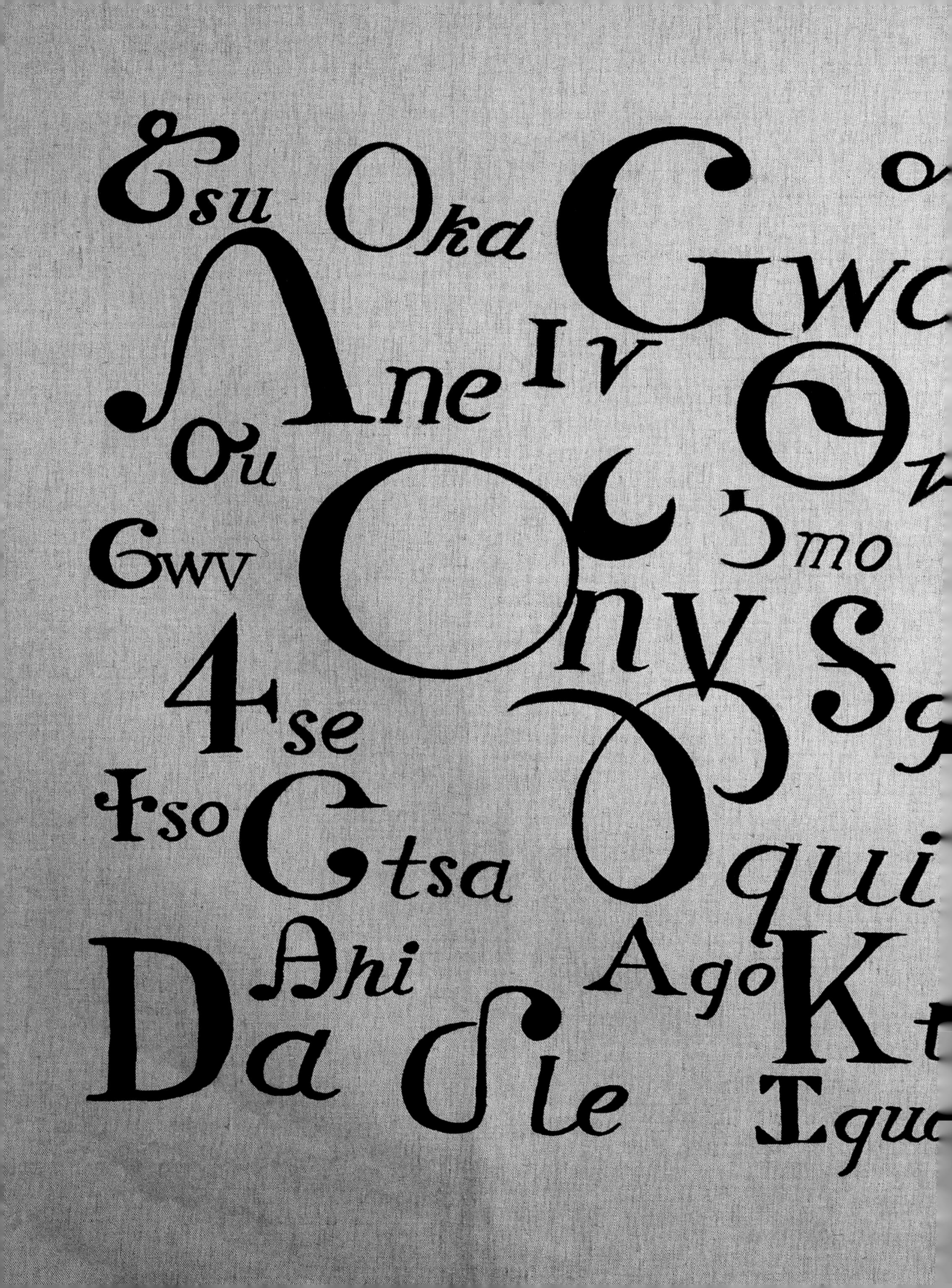